50 Lights:
Innovations in Design and Materials

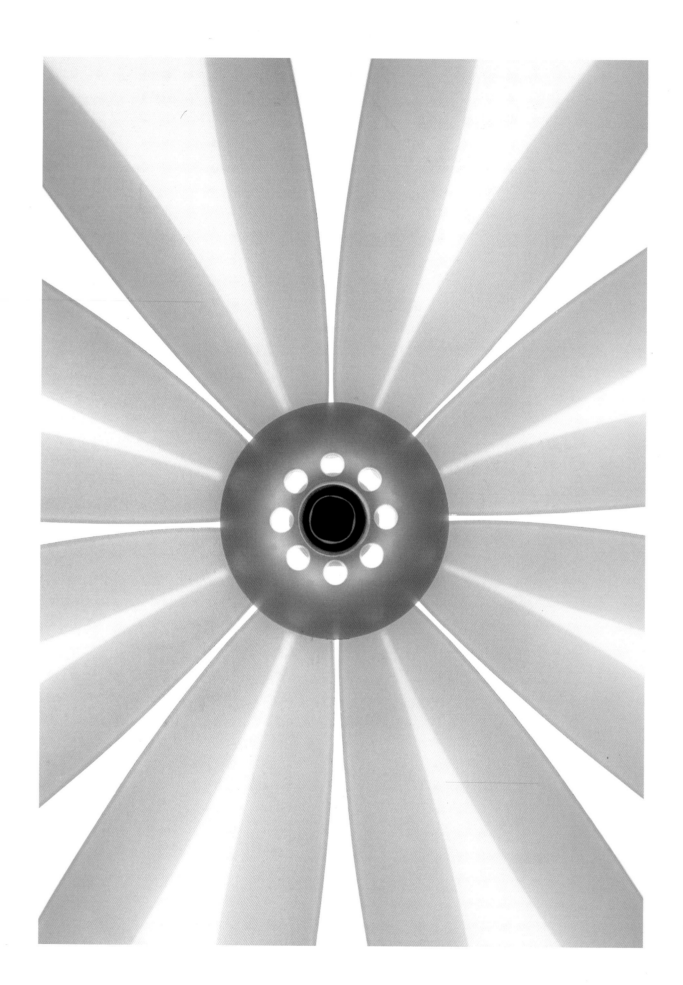

50 LIGHTS

Innovations in Design and Materials

Mel Byars

Introduction by
Paola Antonelli

Research by
Cinzia Anguissola d'Altoé
Brice d'Antras

Technical drawings by
Marvin Fein

A Rotovision Book

PRODESIGN SERIES

 RotoVision

RotoVision

Published by RotoVision SA
Rue du Bugnon, 7
CH-1299 Crans-Près-Céligny
Switzerland

RotoVision SA
Sales & Editorial Office
Sheridan House
112/116A Western Road
Hove East Sussex, BN3 IDD, England
Tel: +44–1273–7272–68
Fax: +44–1273–7272–69

Distributed to the trade in the United States
Watson-Guptill Publications
1515 Broadway
New York, NY 10036
U.S.A.

ISBN 2-88046-265-7

This book was written, designed, and
produced by Mel Byars.

Printed in Singapore

Production and separation
by ProVision Pte. Ltd. Singapore
Tel: +65–334–7720
Fax: +65–334–7721

PRO DESIGN SERIES

50 Chairs: Innovations in Design and Materials
by Mel Byars with an Introduction by Alexander von Vegesack

50 Tables: Innovations in Design and Materials
by Mel Byars with an Introduction by Sylvain Dubuisson

50 Lights: Innovations in Design and Materials
by Mel Byars with an Introduction by Paola Antonelli

50 Products: Innovations in Design and Materials
by Mel Byars with an Introduction by David Revere McFadden

Contents

Introduction:
Of Lamps and Shoes

Contemporary designers have found in technology a precious resource for their poetry; therefore, this book, *50 Lights*, could have been just as easily called *50 Sonnets*.

Today, technology offers designers access to new materials and techniques that they can change and customize at will, a facility that offers them a new exhilarating freedom. Good contemporary designers, like musicians improvising jazz, have learned to take advantage of this new freedom with an elegant nonchalance acquired only through years of strenuous technical exercise. Mel Byars, an acute contemporary observer, describes these virtuoso exercises with a detached approach that allows the beauty of the design process to shine through. At the same time, he makes it possible for a design object and its significance to be easily understood by a wide audience.

Design has been a trade secret for years because too many of its commentators have preferred intellectual distance over communality with the world of things. While good designers struggle to make beautiful things, design critics and historians have felt compelled to elevate these things to the status of well-designed objects. The real world comes back with a vengeance: about a century of industrial-design history shows that only a few well-designed objects have graduated to become beautiful things. This shift in status occurs when design objects become universally understood, appreciated, and used every day by everyone. A gently subversive design critic such as Mel Byars has a way of initiating this process. He focuses his attention on a few selected good objects and then disseminates the simple intellectual joy of revealing how they are made. After his books, *50 Chairs* and *50 Tables*, it is the lamp's turn.

Dutch designer Gijs Bakker once provokingly observed that bulb manufacturers have already done the difficult job, leaving designers simply to dream up ways to conceal the bulb. Therefore, designing a lamp might seem a redundant task. In women's shoe design, for example, one could similarly assert that footwear manufacturers have already performed the difficult job, leaving designers simply to dream up ways of keeping the sole attached to the foot. But, on the contrary, necessity of function coexists with the pure, sensual delight of form and variation, and together they elevate lamps to the status of design fetishes. Some lamps are as painfully gratifying and as impractical as patent-leather, spike-heeled shoes, while some others are as soothing and embracing as a pair of Air Jordans. People buy lamps, just like shoes, to make a stylistic statement. A useful exercise might be to think of the psychological and sociological implications of a crystal chandelier, the "Tizio" desk lamp, or the small plastic *abat-jour* by Philippe Starck. Lamps are a very personal, defining choice.

In a designer's hands, light surely gives our world its definition. For this reason, light has for a very long time obsessed architects who have built the world in its religious adoration. Ever since electricity brought the sun and the moon into our homes 24 hours a day, the obsession spread to interior and industrial designers.

Nothing reaches deeper into a designer's soul than the challenge of creating a lighting fixture. A lamp brings a designer's voice to its lyrical extremes—because it does not have to follow the body's physical limitations, because it allows for a subtle play with translucence and shadow, because it has a hot and luminous core, because it can be made of so many different materials. Chairs and tables, with their gross volumes, may disguise the true nature of a passionate neo-baroque or sensitive minimalist sprit, but lamps don't lie.

With these 50 design tales from the past decade, Mel Byars encompasses the horizon of design at almost the close of the 20th century, when advanced materials and high technology have required a scrupulous craftsman's approach and old-fashioned manufacturing processes have found new life in diversified series and unexpected combinations. At last, the adjective "industrial" is an option, permitting things to reveal, through the process of their making, their modern ethic and their Postmodern individuality.

Paola Antonelli
Associate Curator
Department of Architecture and Design
The Museum of Modern Art
New York

Foreword:
The Ephemeral, Evanescent, Momentary, Transitory, and Disposable

Lighting fixtures are strange animals indeed. When they are turned off, they are still objects that make a statement. And we want them to speak; everything we own speaks of who we are whether we like it or not. Even when we own nothing or very little, a voice makes an announcement.

Unlike other furniture, lamps are not beholden to strict engineering principles. A chair must safely hold its occupant and instill security, even if it is soft or moves, and a table must remain rigid when in use, even if you can see through it, fold it, or roll it away. But a lighting fixture can be ephemeral, evanescent, momentary, transitory, even short lived, disposable. It can be very, very expensive or very, very cheap. The inventory of usable materials at the designers' fingertips appears to be endless: wood, metal, stone, fabric, paper, and—now that certain others have become respectable—a universe of plastics and a macrocosm of remarkable high-tech composites and ceramics. The Japanese have used paper for centuries, even for flame-type illuminators, and a French lamp recently published in a Japanese magazine featured a sconce whose diffuser is pressed seaweed. (pages 114-115).

The possibilities of lamp design and the materials to make fixtures were vastly extended when Thomas Alva Edison invented the incandescent light bulb almost yesterday, in 1879. And the parameters have essentially remained free (with some regulations governing wiring and transformers) until very recently when there began to be the problems created by the halogen bulb: a 500-watt filament has proved to be far too hot, creating fires and thus encouraging the passage of governmental laws, rules, and regulations, resulting in the banning of their use in some countries. And, even though the 300-watt halogen filament is still acceptable, laws will now govern even their use, limiting designers and directly influencing their forms.

Other advances in bulb technology have included the cooler screw-type fluorescent bulb as a substitute for the incandescent version. But, alas, the desire for a decade-long bulb life is still unfulfilled, no doubt due to the Möbius-strip demand of capitalism whose perpetuity demands obsolescence or, in the case of the light bulb,

the death of a product.

With scientific, political, and economic pragmatism aside, this book addresses lighting fixtures as distinct objects, although one example here is merely an illusion (pages 150–151). Therefore, there is no indirect lighting, and few examples concern adjunct lighting systems (like those fitted to tracks or components in open-office plans). Just as a designer often must create chairs with and without arms, lighting fixtures today are often interpreted in versions of a single design in a configuration for placement on a table, the floor, and the wall and from the ceiling. The samples here serve to illustrate the designers' imagination and conceptual thinking.

Unlike tables, chairs, and some other furniture and furnishings, but more like fabrics, the design community and the public are receptive to lighting forms which express flights of fancy that reject severe abstract geometry, call upon real images (like hearts and birds), and express kitsch metaphors (like the use of paper bags that say "paper bag" and translations of traditional fabric-covered lamp shades into forms that have nothing to do with tradition but are merely Postmodernist puns).

As Augusto Morello observes in *Plastiche e Design* (Milano: Arcadia, 1988): "The illuminating object . . . is the one which we can best see the possible decorative redundancy connected with formality—while the dominant function of a lighting instrument is not that of 'shedding light' (which is, perhaps, the task of the bulb or its equivalent) but rather that of lending quality to light . . . "

Thus, this book features lamp designs which Morello suggests are what lighting fixtures are really all about; a lamp is to a bulb as a bridge is to an automobile. Anyone can hang a bare light bulb and socket from a ceiling, just as you can cross a river on any merely adequate bridge.

But hopefully life is served by more than mundane objects; our individual power today may be best or more effectively expressed when we exert control over our own private rooms than when we futilely attempt to effect change over the public environment.

Foreword

Concerning control and choice, the masses have rejected the chastity of 20th-century Modernism time after time; unfortunately, their choice of the opposite or another aesthetic has frequently resulted in the truly dreadful. And they have remained unmoved by the enthusiasm expressed by design historians and journalists for the Modernist idiom. Further, the deliberate vulgarity of some Postmodernist retro-expressions has ridiculed the taste of the masses and fostered their resentment, whether they are consciously aware of their enmity or not.

Contrarily, good design with wide appeal does verily exist in great quantity, if you will excuse my arrogant assumption that I know what is "good" and "bad" while acknowledging the vast amount of published commentary on the subject. An amalgamation of purity and artifice has been nowhere more vivaciously expressed than in Italy where native and foreign designers have united with manufacturers and technicians in a symbiotic symphony. Even though the result of their coalition has been imaginative, even delightful, the situation handicaps a book like this whose imperative is international in scope. The flow and bulk of good design in Italy has been profuse since the 1950s, although today the paranoid and fiercely nationalist design community there is being unjustly alarmed by competition, especially from Britain.

Nevertheless, worldwide coverage has been seditiously attempted in this book, though the Japanese proved diffident if not indifferent and certainly unresponsive, maybe even haughty. This survey is the result of the amenable, generous, and patient manufacturers and designers who furnished the images and information you find here. The book is blessed by having Brice d'Antras and Cinzia Anguissola d'Altoé contribute to the gathering of material; they are highly competent independent scholars in their own right and far more knowledgeable and energetic than I. Even though now the book exists as a tangible object and its organization and nature is presumably obvious, it was difficult for us to describe the project in advance. Explaining an idea is always a problem when it is a yet-to-be-realized scheme with no or few primogenitors.

A concerted effort was made to feature the work of both male and female designers of all races and from all continents which necessarily and happily includes a range of interpretations expressing various worldviews but often available riches or poverty.

The book is not an advertising medium. No one remunerated the publisher or author as an incentive for inclusion; the materials were donated free of charge for publication. No nepotism and no special favors were extended. No suggestion is being made that you should purchase any object here nor that you need any of them; you do not.

To repeat, you can always hang a bare bulb from the ceiling with the cord running down the wall. After all, for millennia people used raw firelight to see in places that were dark. For only a century and a quarter have we used electricity at, it might be noted, a very great price—expensive both in money and as a detractor to the environment. But, alack, we are addicts.

Mel Byars
New York City

Metals

"Marie" table light

Designer: Jorge Pensi (Argentine, b. 1946)
Manufacturer: B.Lux, Bizbaia, Spain
Date of design: 1990
Bulb: two halogen, 20w, 12v

An innovative design, the raising and lowering of the bulb head is made possible by the double-rod pedestal; one rod is wired for the positive pole of electrical and the other for the negative pole. Thus, no matter the position of the head, electrical current is provided to the bulb. (For a similar positive-negative wiring configuration, see pages 102–103.)

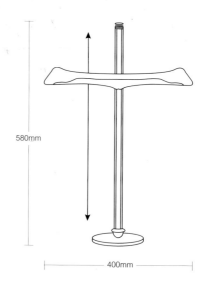

580mm

400mm

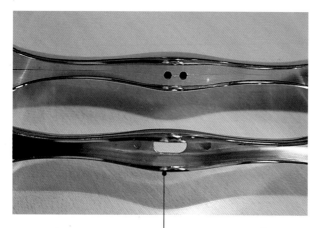

The housing for the bulb is cast aluminum.

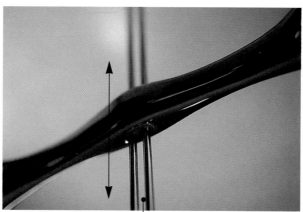

The bulb housing (wired so that each of the two pedestal rods serves as either negative or positive electrical poles) can be moved up or down.

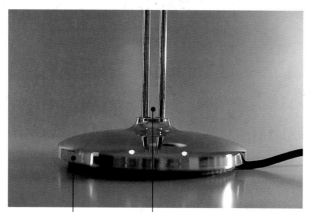

The base is cast aluminum.

The positive and negative pedestal rods enter the base.

The underside view of the weighted base.

"Jet" table and wall light

Designer: J. Garcia Garay (Argentine, b. 1945)
Manufacturer: Garcia Garay S.L., Barcelona,
Spain
Date of design: 1990
Bulb: E14 incandescent, 60w, 220–240v

An example of the work of one of a number
of Argentine designers working and living in
Spain, this fixture was configured to fold, making
shipment cheaper. When a plate is added, wall
mounting is possible. About a 1,000 examples
of this lamp are produced annually by the
designer/entrepreneur.

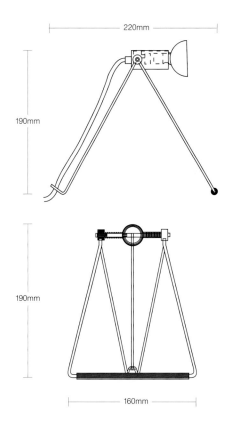

Stainless-steel springs
provide tension while
allowing for 360° rotation
of the bulb housing.

Except for the aluminum
bulb housing and stainless-
steel springs, all parts are
chromium-plated brass rods.

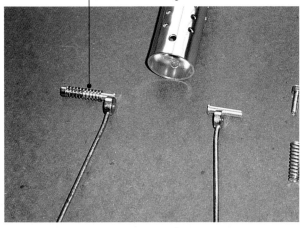

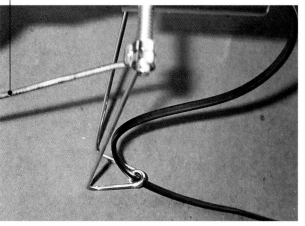

The bulb housing is anodized aluminum
to better dissipate the bulb heat.

The axle attached to the bulb housing
and the legs, allows for 360° rotation with
tension to keep the housing stationary.

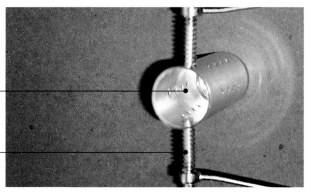

"Au Pair" sconce

Designer: Donald Stählin (Swiss, b. 1960)
Manufacturer: the designer
Date of design: 1989
Bulb: halogen, 12v, 50w

The elements of this sconce are essentially unaltered functional objects not ordinarily used in lighting construction. This Dadaistic foray is an exercise more about whimsey than recycling. The name, "Au pair," is play on words making references to the architect-designer's using a pair of aluminum shoe trees to form a pair of lighting fixtures. Each of the sconces is owned by a different person.

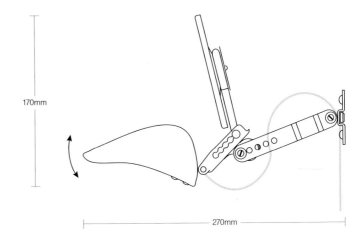

Light from the adjustable shoe tree, which already had a hinge in its original state, produces a dramatic effect on the wall, projected through the diffuser (a vegetable strainer).

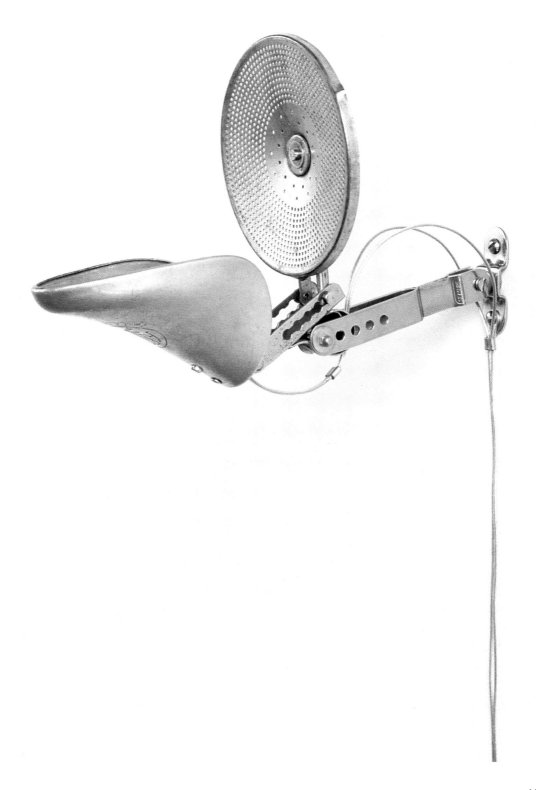

"Au Pair" sconce

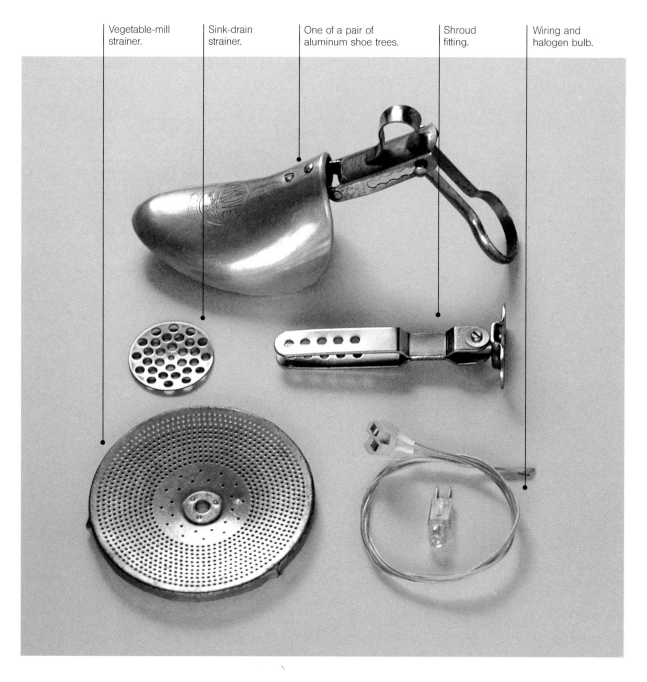

Vegetable-mill strainer.

Sink-drain strainer.

One of a pair of aluminum shoe trees.

Shroud fitting.

Wiring and halogen bulb.

A view exposing the halogen bulb (12v, 50w) in the downwardly tilted shoe tree.

"Kri" hanging lights

Designer: Asahara Sigheaki (Japanese, b. 1948)
Manufacturer: Lucitalia S.p.A., Cinisello Bergamo (MI), Italy
Date of design: 1994
Bulbs: dichroic halogen, 35mm or 50mm diameter; 12v; 20w, 35w, or 50w; toroidal or electronic transformers of different powers

Different stem lengths, and wall and pedestal mounting lend wide functional possibilities to this lighting system. Since the accessories (sleeve and diffuser) are on a stem, dichroic bulbs may be used. The stem can be attached to rail tracks, ceiling plates (with or without a transformer for single or three-spot mounting), connectors for linear metal plank ceiling, wall connectors, and other connectors.

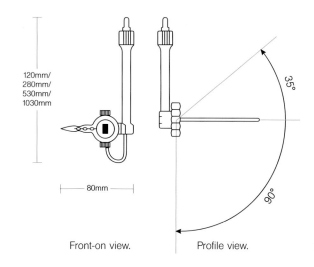

120mm/
280mm/
530mm/
1030mm

80mm

35°

90°

Front-on view.

Profile view.

Extruded aluminum screen (seven colors).

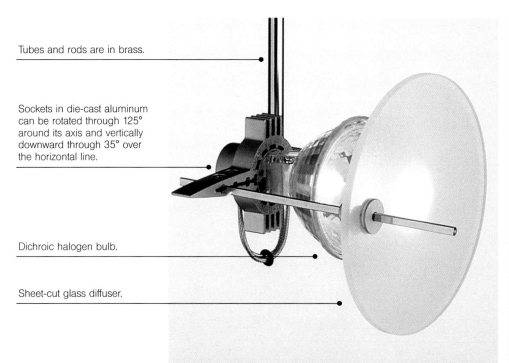

Tubes and rods are in brass.

Sockets in die-cast aluminum can be rotated through 125° around its axis and vertically downward through 35° over the horizontal line.

Dichroic halogen bulb.

Sheet-cut glass diffuser.

The system may be fitted with or without screens or diffusers.

"X135" table light

Designer: Gaspar Glusberg (Argentine, b. 1959)
Manufacturer: modulor S.A., Buenos Aires, Argentina
Date of design: 1994
Bulb: dichroic, 50w, 220–12v, with a standard transformer (50w, 220–12v) in the body.

The internal bearing element of this fixture together with an intermediate acrylic ring permits the rotation of the bulb housing and thus the projected light. Though different in its essential mechanics, compare this example with the glass-bottom lamp on pages 106–110.

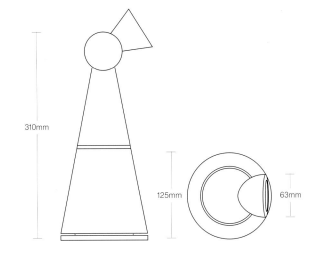

310mm

125mm   63mm

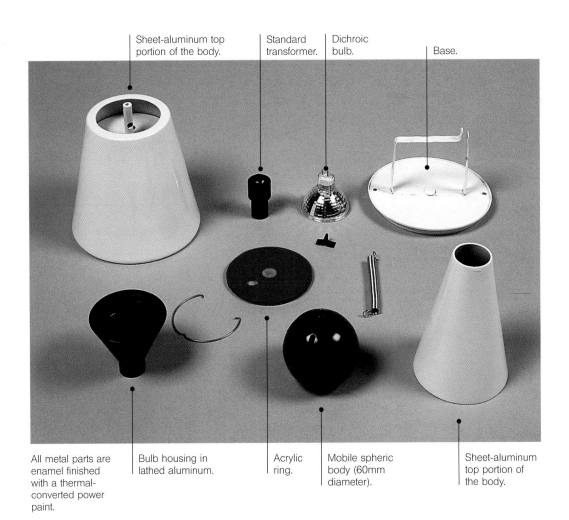

Sheet-aluminum top portion of the body.

Standard transformer.

Dichroic bulb.

Base.

All metal parts are enamel finished with a thermal-converted power paint.

Bulb housing in lathed aluminum.

Acrylic ring.

Mobile spheric body (60mm diameter).

Sheet-aluminum top portion of the body.

"Heron" table light

Designer: Isao Hosoe (Japanese, b. 1942)
Manufacturer: Luxo Italiana S.p.A., Presezzo
(Bergamo), Italy
Date of design: 1994
Bulb: GY6–35 halogen, 50w, 12v; 50w transformer
in the base

A result of the cooperation of the designer and
the technical staff of the manufacturer, this lamp
features small wheels on the bottom surface that
permit its easy movement on a flat surface. The
reflector, more or less the head of the abstracted
"heron," remains parallel to the work surface
when its height is altered. The body is made of
glass-reinforced PA66 (nylon).

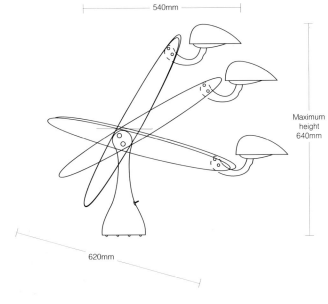

540mm

Maximum
height
640mm

620mm

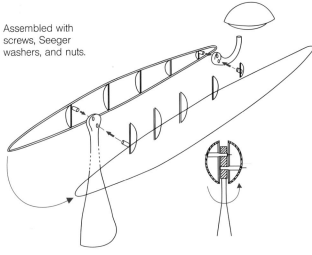

Assembled with
screws, Seeger
washers, and nuts.

Available in black, white,
and metallic colors: silver,
yellow, blue, and red.

"Heron" table light

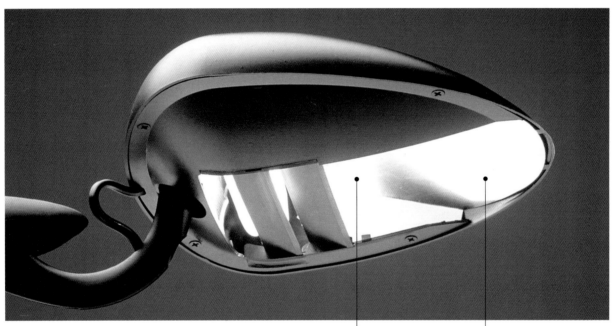

The reflector is high-polished aluminum.

Pyrex protective glass.

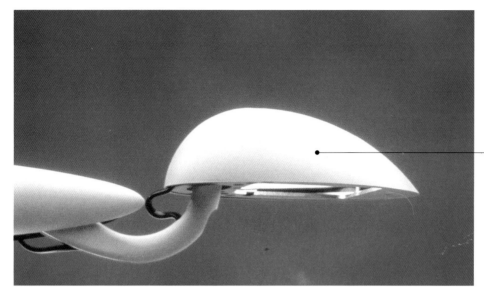

The reflector head remains parallel to the work surface when the height is changed.

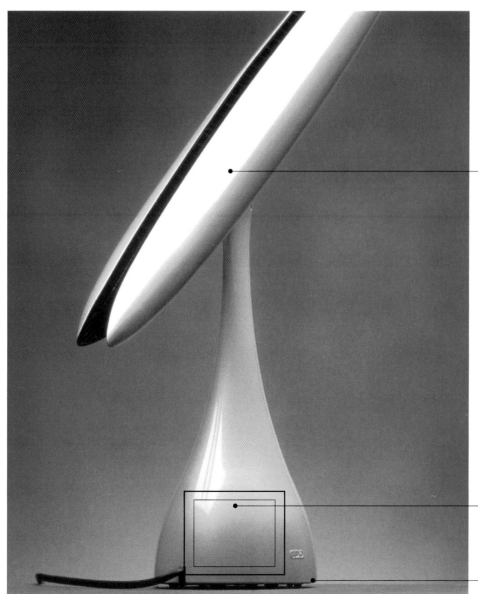

The arm and body are glass-reinforced PA66 (nylon).

A 50w transformer is built into the base.

Small wheels (polycarbonate, covered with silicon rubber) on the bottom of the base allow for easy surface movement.

6

"Heron" table light

A preliminary drawing by the designer.

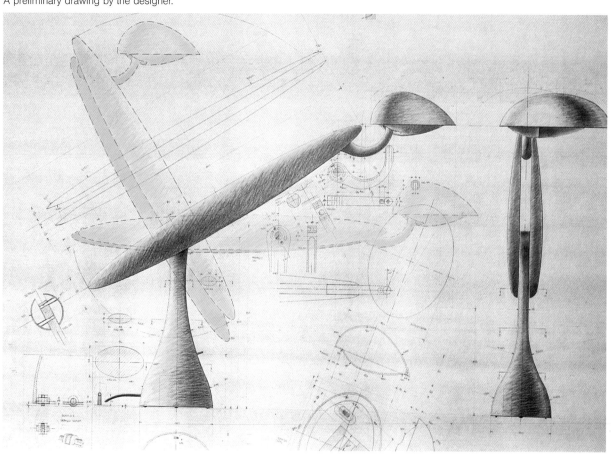

"Zen" light

Designers: Sergi Devesa i Bajet (Spanish,
b. 1961) and Oscar Devesa i Bajet (Spanish,
b. 1963)
Manufacturer: Melalarte S.A., Barcelona, Spain
Date of design: 1989
Bulb: E14 incandescent, 25w

More a fetish than a functional lighting fixture,
the name of this lamp reveals its inspirations: the
Orient, Kendo masks, and the Zibalinga of Doctor
Jones. It ignores the demands of arriving at a
specific design solution, providing, as the
designers have suggested, "an effect of warmth
and mystery." Using Zamac metal, this light is
heavy for its size and extra weighted at the
bottom to prevent its tipping over.

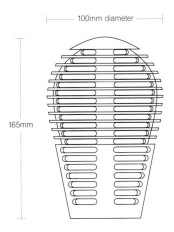

100mm diameter

165mm

Injection-molded Zamac (an
aluminum-like metal, but much
heavier) is formed into two
equal halves held by small
male prongs on one side that fit
female receptacles on the other.

The metal surface is brushed.

A polycarbonate screen filters
the light and provides a certain
ethereal effect.

The two equal halves of the
body are connected by the
use of Allen screws and a
screwdriver.

"Zen" light

The on/off switch is built into the body of the fixture.

The electrical cord enters the body through a rubber gasket.

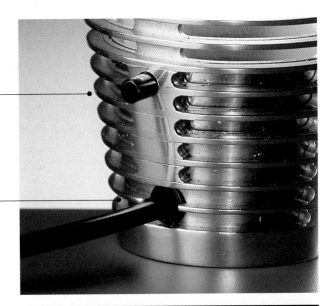

Molded sides before trimming.

With the appearance of the mysterious object that the designers intended, the fixture glows in the dark.

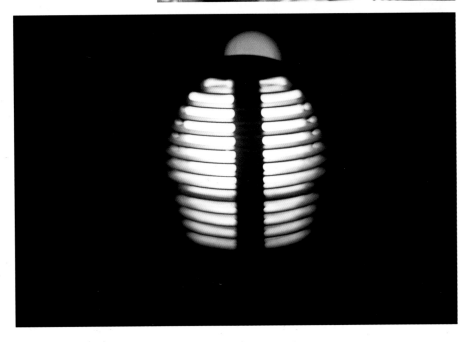

"Loto" floor and table lights

Designer: Guglielmo Berchicci (Italian,
b. 1957)
Manufacturer: Kundalini S.r.l., Milano, Italy
Date of design: 1997
Bulb: E27 halotube, or E14 incandescent,
or 150w energy saving, 110–120v

Two different ovoid-shaped polycarbonate
strips are attached onto plastic rings to form
a lighted pod, whose shape can be changed
by sliding a plastic ring on the lamp's stem.
The superstructure is a traditional floor lamp
structure to which an imaginative diffuser
configuration has been added.

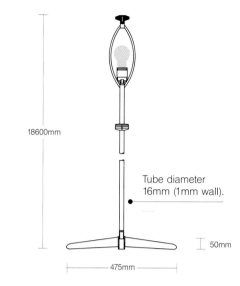

18600mm

Tube diameter
16mm (1mm wall).

50mm

475mm

The three views of the same lamp illustrate
how the lighting pod can be reshaped
when a polycarbonate ring is slid upward
on the main stem.

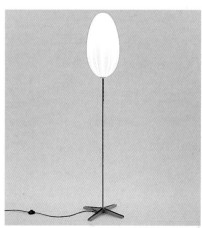

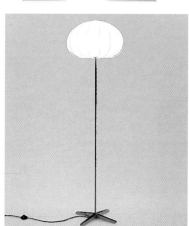

"Loto" floor and table lights

Alternating eight large serigraphic painted polycarbonate ovoid strips (677mm x 112mm) composing half of the diffuser.

Alternating eight small serigraphic painted polycarbonate ovoid strips (654mm x 101mm) composing the other half of the diffuser.

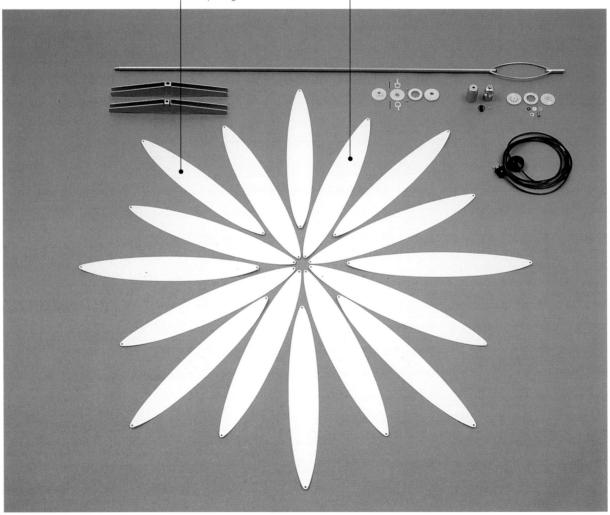

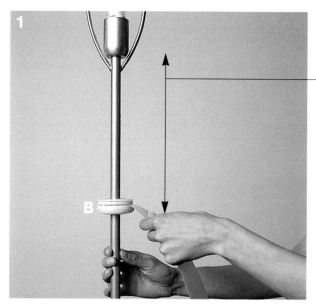

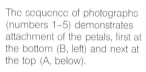

When all the polycarbonate petals are attached to the die-cast polycarbonate rings (A and B), the pod shape of the petals can be changed when the bottom (B) is slid upward toward the top (A; see photo 3).

The sequence of photographs (numbers 1–5) demonstrates attachment of the petals, first at the bottom (B, left) and next at the top (A, below).

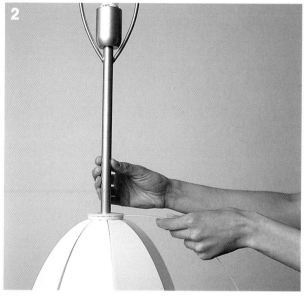

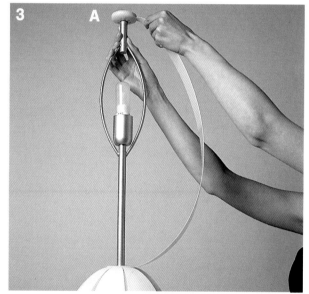

"Borealis" bollard

Designers: Perry King (British, b. 1938)
and Santiago Miranda (Spanish, b. 1947)
Manufacturer: Louis Poulsen & Co. A/S,
Copenhagen, Denmark
Date of design: 1996
Bulb: E27, 50–100w; GX24d-3, 26w

Intended for use in gardens, parks, and other
public areas, the form of this bollard was
inspired by a photograph of the common
comfrey by the German pedagogue Karl
Blossfeldt. This fixture incorporates a plastic
diffuser and an aluminum base; an aluminum
reflector is housed inside the clear version of
the diffuser.

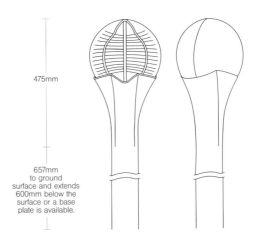

475mm

657mm
to ground
surface and extends
600mm below the
surface or a base
plate is available.

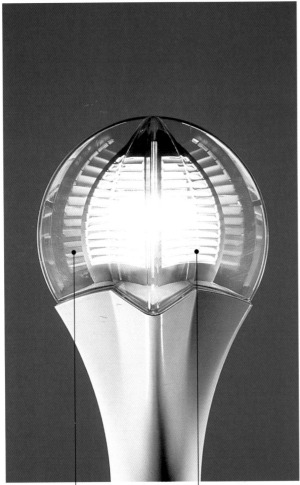

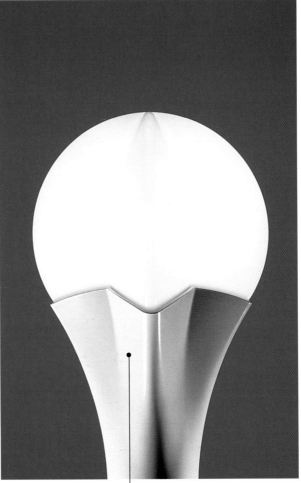

Inside the clear version
of the diffuser are
reflective inner shields
of metal-lacquered
aluminum.

Both clear and
opalescent versions
of the diffuser are
injection-molded
polycarbonate.

The post is white or
gray enamel-painted
extruded aluminum.

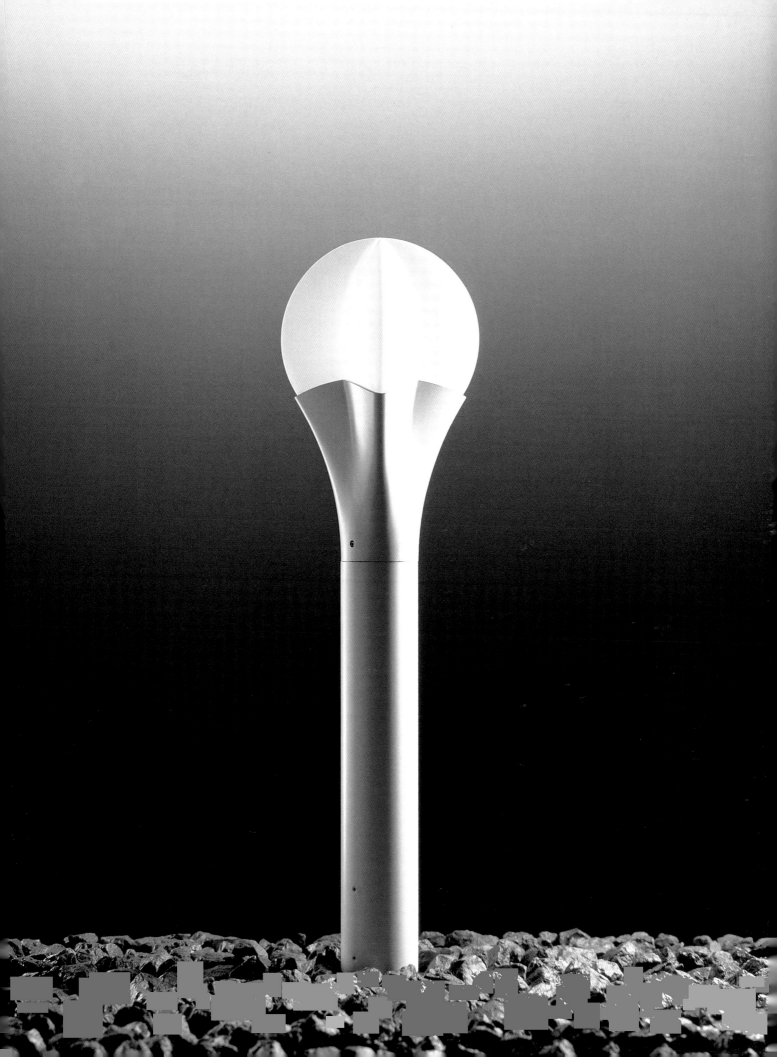

"Borealis" bollard

The photographs of the flowering maple (*Abutilon*), top, and the common comfrey (*Symphytum officinale*), bottom right, are two of thousands obsessively taken by Karl Blossfeldt (1865–1932). The photographer, plant collector, and pedagogue, for 31 years from 1899 as an instructor at the Charlottenburg-Berlin Kunstgewerbe-schule, used his images to demonstrate that the best human-created industrial forms had already been accomplished in nature. Notice that the flowering maple pod (right), when inverted, shows an intensional commonality with the form of the "Borealis" diffuser.

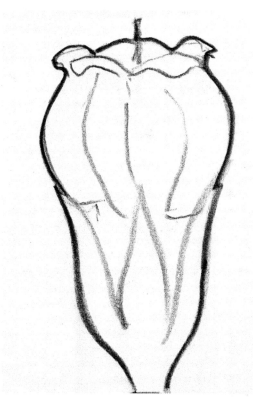

The designers' drawing intreprets the Blossfeldt photograph of the common comfrey.

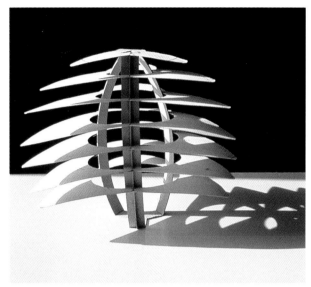

Maquettes here inform early developmental stages of the lamp's diffuser. The example in the upper-right corner reveals influences of the manufacturer's famous lamps by Poul Henningensen (1894–1967).

"Borealis" bollard

The fixture has been installed in the plaza of La Defense in Paris, France. (See the top of the facing page.)

A disassembled fixture with a clear diffuser.

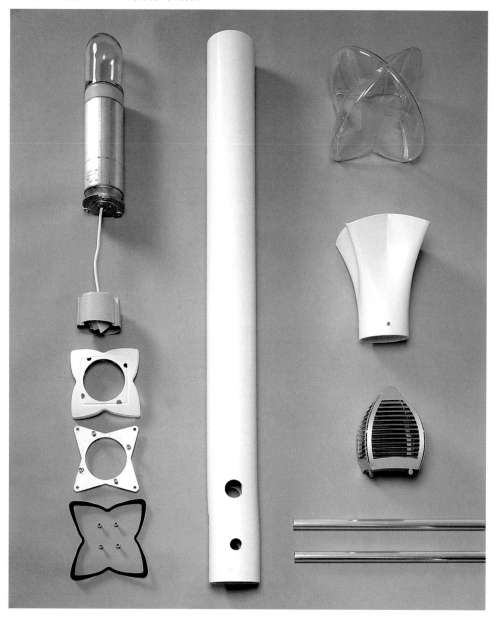

10

"Aphid AlluminANT" light

Designer: Marc Harrison (New Zealander, b. 1970)
Manufacturer: ANTworks, Moorooka, Australia
Date of design: 1994
Bulb: table version: SBC incandescent 40w, sconce: 75w compact fluorescent

Respecting both the traditional and the advanced in the use of materials, this fixture deftly combines wood and plastic. This insect-like lamp was designed in two different versions, for the table-top surface and for the wall and is easily portable serving what the designer describes as "stationary and nomadic lifestyles."

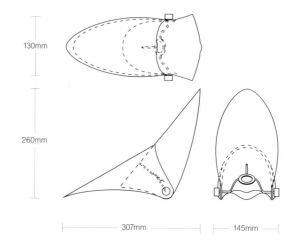

130mm

260mm

307mm   145mm

This lamp is assembled and made with a press and CNC (computer numeric controlled) router and employs fastenings and fittings in stainless-steel—the sconce parts at top and the table version at bottom.

The body is in wood from the locale of the production, Australia.

Compact fluorescent bulb (top) and incandescent bulb (bottom).

The diffuser is in polycarbonate sheeting.

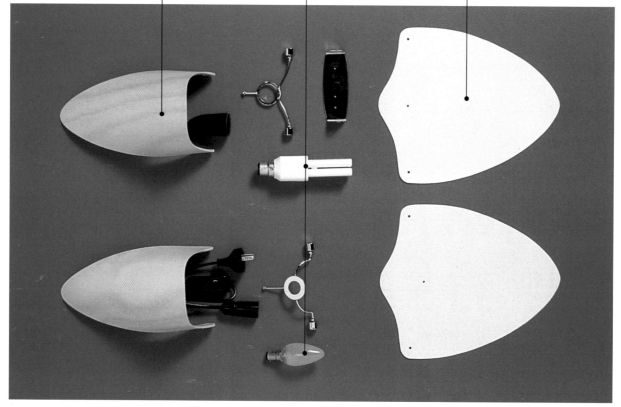

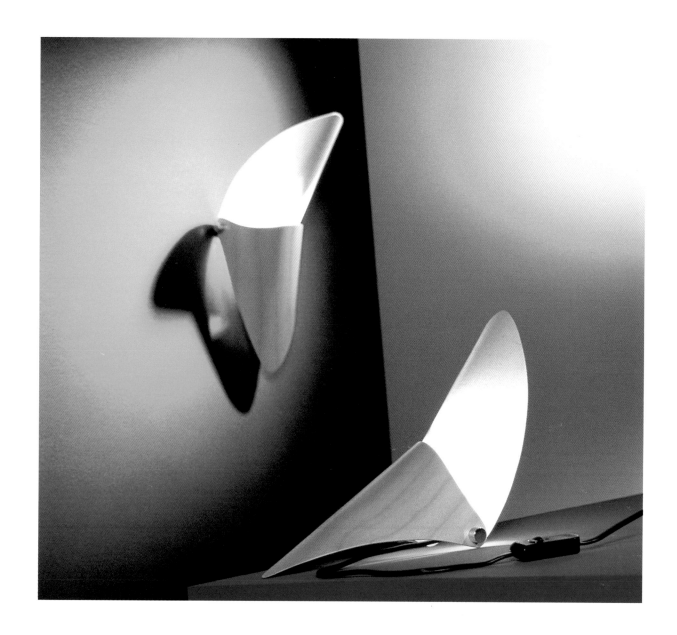

11

"Madame Ruby" table light

Designers: Celina Clarke (Australian, b. 1967)
and Simon Christopher (Australian, b. 1967)
Manufacturer: ISM Objects, South Melbourne,
Victoria, Australia
Date of design: 1994
Bulb: incandescent candle, 25w

An industrious essay in recycling, this table lamp
employs the use of discarded and reprocessed
plastic parts from automobiles and other
products. The lighting fixture, not particularly
bright due to a 25w-maximum bulb, nevertheless emits a particularly brilliant glow due to
the characteristics of the original materials.

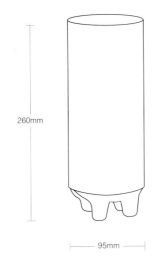

260mm

95mm

The percentage of the mixture of polycarbonate and acrylic plastics, like those
of discarded automobile tail lights, varies
in the composite recycling process.

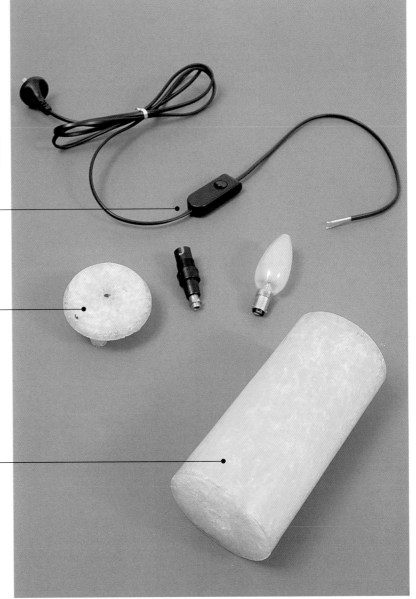

The on/off switch is
electrical-line attached.

The base is
attached to the
body with bolts.

The body, like the
base, made of
recycled plastics
has an opening in
the top to permit
heat escapage.

The lamp employs
standard electrical
parts.

12

"UFO" hanging light

Designer: Nick Crosbie (British, b. 1971)
Manufacturer: Inflate, London, England
Date of design: 1996

This lamp is a particularly intriguing object due to its obvious inflated nature and to its marriage of a hot electrical bulb with a fragile, thin plastic film. The fixture is furnished to the end user in a plastic bag with instructions for assembly. The lamp is available in a range of bright colors that also appear in the design firm/manufacturer's other products that include egg cups, other lighting fixtures, fruit bowls, chairs, and wine racks.

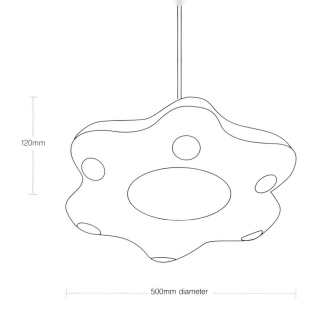

120mm

500mm diameter

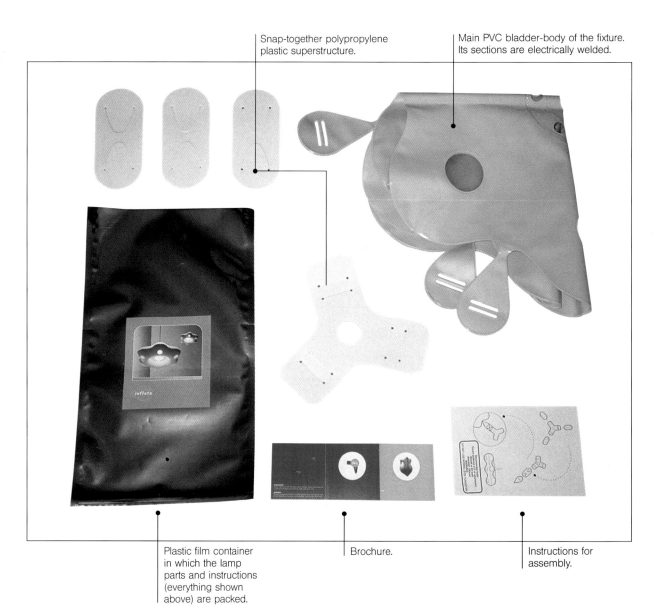

Snap-together polypropylene plastic superstructure.

Main PVC bladder-body of the fixture. Its sections are electrically welded.

Plastic film container in which the lamp parts and instructions (everything shown above) are packed.

Brochure.

Instructions for assembly.

13

"Urchin" light

Designer: Jonathan Goldman (American, b. 1959)
Manufacturer: Goldman Arts, Inc., Belmont, Massachusetts
Date of design: 1989
Bulb: A19 incandescent, 75w, 110v

The inflated section of this fixture is made of thin rip-stop nylon fabric. Larger than it appears in the photograph, this lamp, if it is indeed a lighting fixture, is both intriguing and whimsical. The fan that expands the spiked diffuser serves both to infuse it with air and to reduce the heat caused by the bulb.

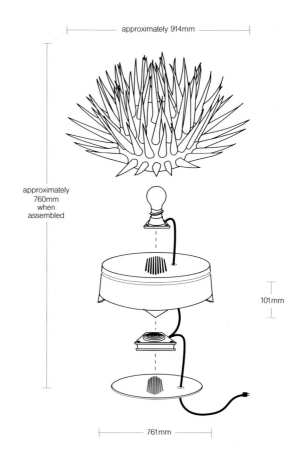

approximately 914mm

approximately 760mm when assembled

101mm

761mm

The diffuser, deflated in this view, is made of rip-stop coated nylon.

The particle-board base, supporting the ceramic bulb socket, is slit-perforated to allow air from the fan below to be blown upward.

The axial fan (110CFM AC) blows air through the slits in the light-bulb base into the nylon diffuser and also cools the unit.

14

"Estação da Luz"

Designers: Luciana Martins (Brazilian,
b. 1967) and Gerson de Oliveira (Brazilian,
b. 1970)
Manufacturer: various local small-scale
shops; assembly by the designers
Date of design: 1995
Bulb: incandescent, 15w

Expandable from three to as many as 20
illuminated units, the most popular configurations range from three to seven boxes.
The designers, who name their objects
using plays on words, call this fixture,
in English, "Station of the Light."
The Portuguese word *estação* means
both station (like railroad station) and
season (as in the four seasons of a year).

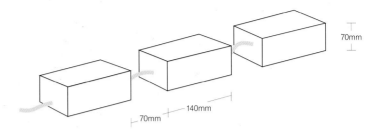

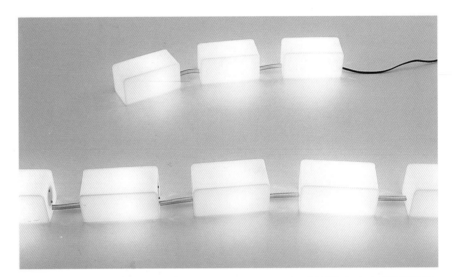

A sheet of acrylic sheeting (4mm
thick) is cut and bent into "U"-
shaped sections. Drilled holes allow
for the insertion of the electrical
wires and also for cooling ventilation.

The bulb socket is screwed into
the end of the acrylic box.

The two sides of the box are
mortised together in a positive/
negative manner but can be
opened for bulb replacement.

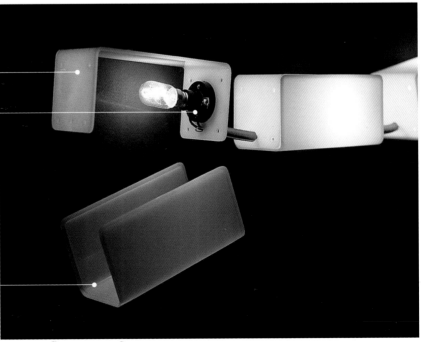

15

"Liquid Light"

Designer: Jean-Marie Massaud
(French, b. 1966)
Manufacturer: prototypes (3) sponsored
by V.I.A., Paris, France
Date of design: 1995
Bulb: compact fluorescent, 11w,
220v; or incandescent, 60w, 220v

Produced in a small quantity as part of
the semi-governmental V.I.A. designer-
manufacturer sponsorship program, this
highly imaginative lamp design features
a bulb that floats in a tinted liquid. It
appears to be more of a strange biological
laboratory experiment than a lighting fixture.
The designer describes the lamp as being
the "fluide de vie" ("fluid of life").

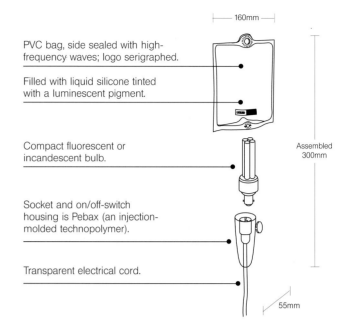

PVC bag, side sealed with high-
frequency waves; logo serigraphed.

Filled with liquid silicone tinted
with a luminescent pigment.

Compact fluorescent or
incandescent bulb.

Socket and on/off-switch
housing is Pebax (an injection-
molded technopolymer).

Transparent electrical cord.

160mm

Assembled
300mm

55mm

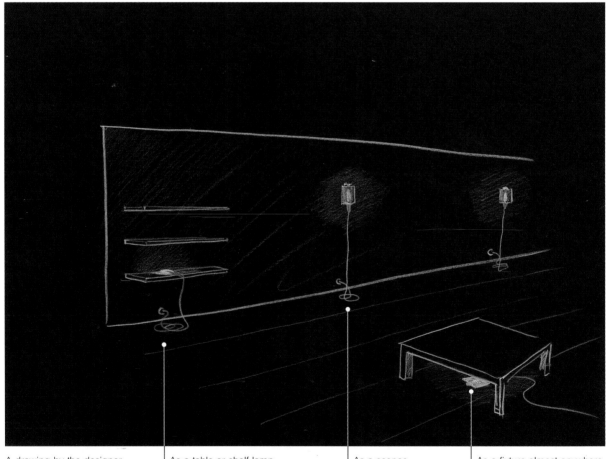

A drawing by the designer
on black paper illustrates
the various applications
of the fixture and its
mobile nature.

As a table or shelf lamp.

As a sconce.

As a fixture almost anywhere.

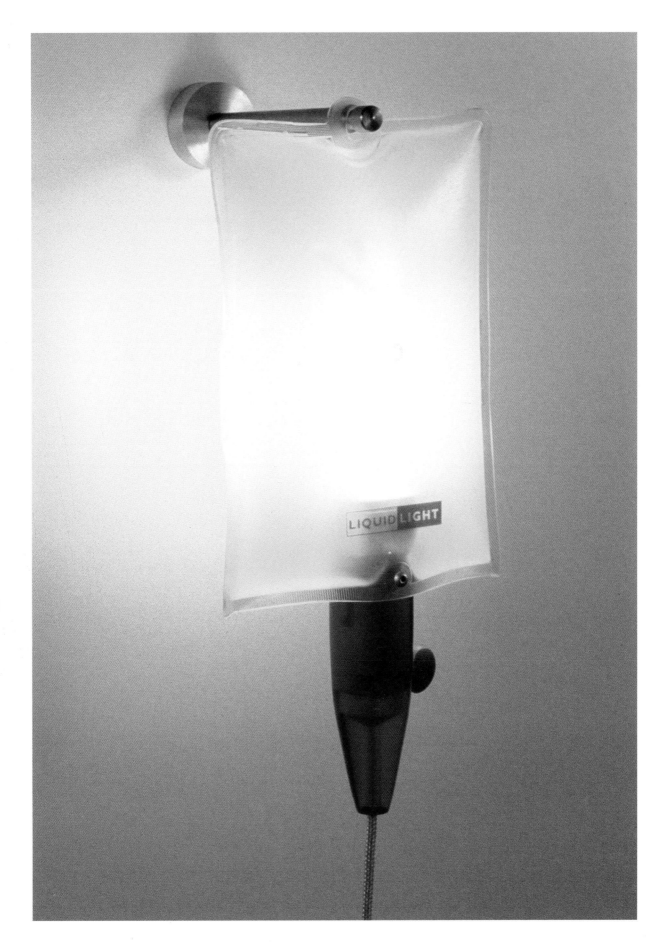

"Titania" table light

Designers: Alberto Meda (Italian, b. 1945) and
Paolo Rizzatto (Italian, b. 1941)
Manufacturer: Luceplan S.p.A., Milano, Italy
Date of design: 1990
Bulb: Osram 250T10 (medium-base double-
envelope frosted halogen), 250w, 115–220v

When someone looks straight on at this lamp
from a distance as close as 1100mm, the
numerous blades of this fixture screen the bulb
and its glare from view. This lamp successfully
combines technological innovation with a certain whimsical lightheartedness, although its
designers may disagree, claiming a far more
serious intent and content.

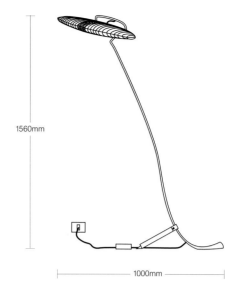

1560mm

1000mm

Available as a
ceiling or floor
model, the latter
is shown here. A
foot-weighted
stand was designed
to suspend what
is essentially the
ceiling version.

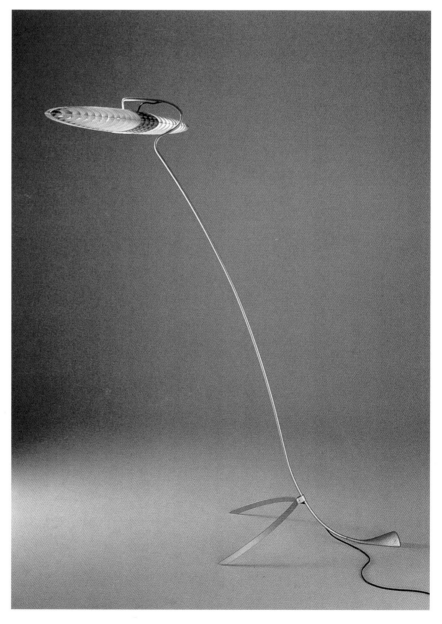

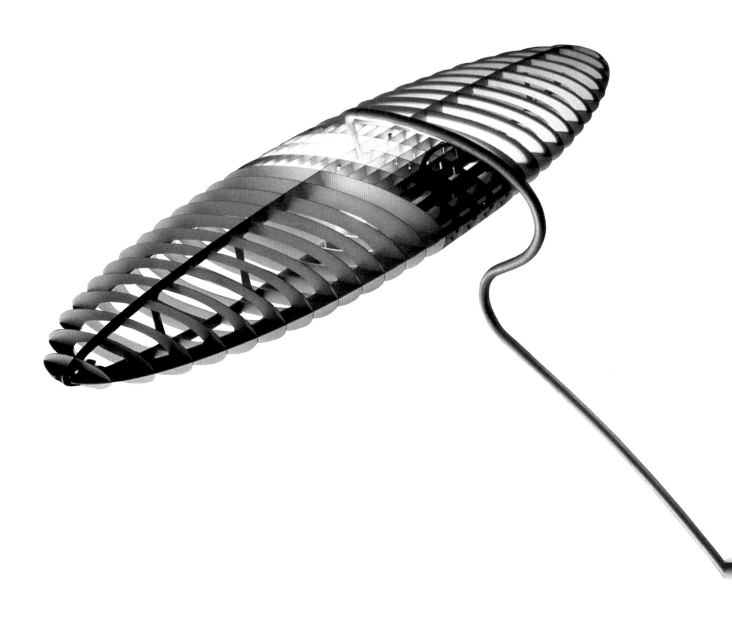

"Titania" table light

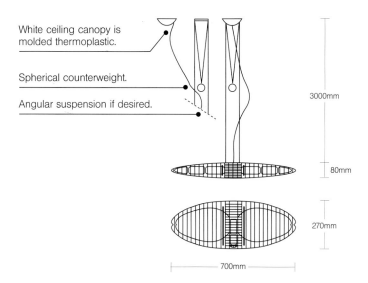

White ceiling canopy is molded thermoplastic.

Spherical counterweight.

Angular suspension if desired.

3000mm

80mm

270mm

700mm

A partially disassembled lamp. The assembly, except that by the end user, is riveted.

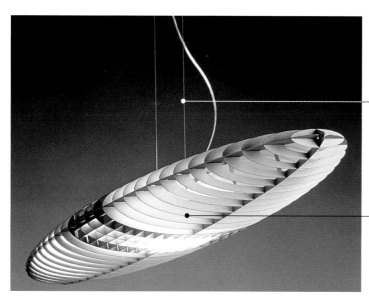

The ceiling model suspends the lamp on two thin nylon strands, separate from the electrical cord. The height is regulated by a ceiling bracket support, balanced by a cast-aluminum counterweight. The two nylon cords permit the fixture to be angled, if desired.

The minor or traversal elliptical ribs range from 270mm x 80mm to 80mm x 25mm in size. They have four slots, at each end and each side to slide onto the major elliptical ribs (see below).

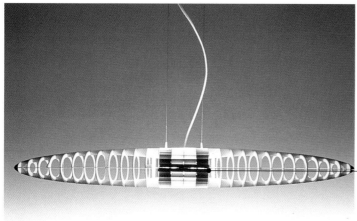

The body is available in a natural or black anodized finish.

Pairs (on each side of the bulb) of interchangeable colored polycarbonate filters (violet, yellow, blue, red, and green) can be employed to create different visual effects at the user's whim.

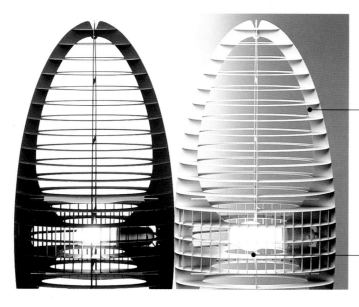

The first set of major elliptical ribs (stamped from aluminum) are placed on the longitudinal plane of the major axis of more than 700mm and minor axis of 270mm. They have numerous slits cut into the sides to accommodate the 24 minor ribs.

The second set of major elliptical ribs are placed on the longitudinal plane of the major axis of more than 700mm and minor axis of 270mm. They also have numerous slits to hold the minor ribs.

17

"Anemone" table light

Designer: Ross Tuthill Menuez (American,
b. 1965)
Manufacturer: Handeye, Inc., Brooklyn, NY, U.S.A.
Date of design: 1996
Bulb: A19 incandescent, 150w

The designer of this fixture is known for his use
of unorthodox materials not normally associated
with the production of high-design furnishings.
Nevertheless, this striking design is distinctive
and, possibly most importantly, emits a pleasant,
ambient glow. The overlapping of the nylon strip
is purposefully irregular.

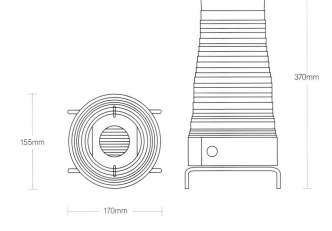

155mm

170mm

370mm

Zytel 42 (nylon) (0.775mm thick
x 152m long). The mill finish is
retained.

The armature and support plate
(hand-brushed nickel-plated
steel) are welded together.

18

"Molle" table light

Designer: Christophe Pillet (French, b. 1959)
Manufacturer: E+Y, Tokyo, Japan
Date of design: 1995
Bulb: compact fluorescent, 11w, 220v

This lamp incorporates the new application of a technologically interesting, though not necessarily new, material: latex. To draw the corollary of the lamp to a human arm because of its skin and the wrist-like flexing may be too obvious. This fixture, made in Japan, exemplifies the kind of international machinations designers endure today. Its inventiveness was recognized by the awards committee of the 30th Salon du luminaire in Paris, France.

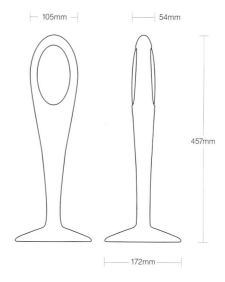

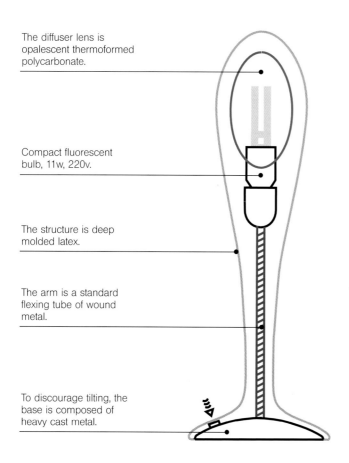

The diffuser lens is opalescent thermoformed polycarbonate.

Compact fluorescent bulb, 11w, 220v.

The structure is deep molded latex.

The arm is a standard flexing tube of wound metal.

To discourage tilting, the base is composed of heavy cast metal.

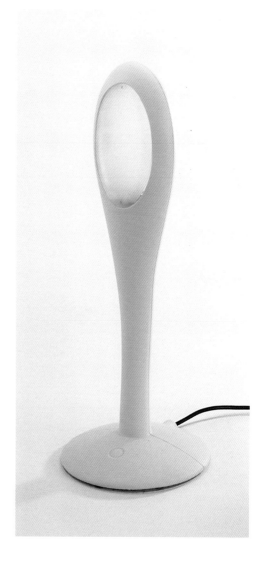

19

"Clips" table light

Designer: Bernard Vuarnesson (French, b. 1935)
Manufacturer: Sculptures-Jeux S.A., Paris, France
Date of design: 1996
Bulb: incandescent frosted golf ball, 40w, 110–220v

While the concept is lighthearted, the execution
is well engineered. The end user may attach any
beverage can of his choosing; as no can is
included with the essential components: the
attachment device, the socket-and-wiring piece,
and the partially recycled shade.

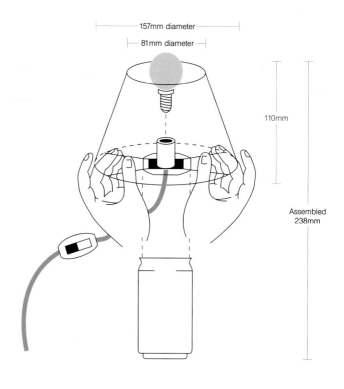

The shade is PVC or
polypropylene (40%
partially recycled)
sheeting (black,
yellow, blue, or red).

The proprietary stainless-steel
clamping device, pre-fixed
to the bottom of the shade,
is attached to the top edge
of a beverage can.

Any standard-size (30cl)
can is suitable. An empty
can should be washed
and, for stability, filled
with sand, rice, etc.

"Wings" table light

Designer: Riccardo Raco (Italian, b. 1952)
Manufacturer: Stamp, a product of Samuel
Parker S.r.l., Pomezia (RO), Italy
Date of design: 1994–95
Bulb: E14 incandescent, 60w, no transformer

This lamp is sold singly and, in order for
the user to create the "wings" effect, in pairs.
Made in a patented plastic material known
as Opalflex, the manufacturer claims it has
the appearance and some of the features of
opaline glass. Its maleability makes it a very
versatile material. This fixture, boxed flat, is
very inexpensive.

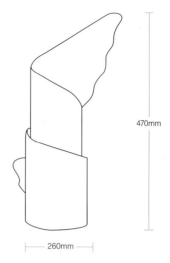

470mm

260mm

Opalflex, a proprietary plastic-vitreous sheet, does not turn yellow and has
special flexing, modeling, and lighting-diffusing characteristics.

For each lamp, one piece of
Opalflex (cut with a machine
especially for the product) is
wound around 2 1/2 times to
form the shape with its wing-
like extension.

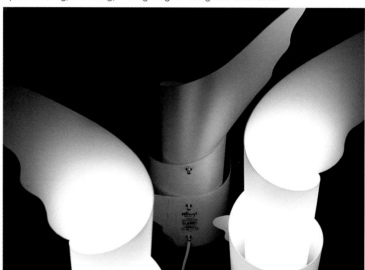

For best results, a 60w milk-
white incandescent or low-
consumption-type bulb is
recommended. Colored bulbs
will create interesting effects.

Three brass screws hold
the one-piece diffuser to
the socket/wiring/base unit.

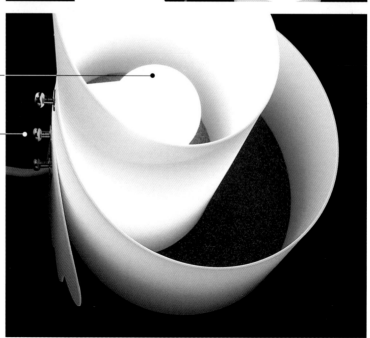

"Drop 1" and "Drop 2" sconces

Designer: Marc Sadler (French, b. 1946)
Manufacturer: Flos S.p.A., Bovezzo (BR), Italy
Date of design: 1992
Bulb: compact fluorescent, 230v (one in "Drop 1" and two in "Drop 2")

The sconce is intriguing to the touch. To maintain the bulb, the diffuser of these lamps can be easily removed by pulling them away from the wall-mounted base. Because the base is transparent, although it does not appear so, light is also projected through the base and onto the wall. Two sizes, each with a different diffuser pattern, are available.

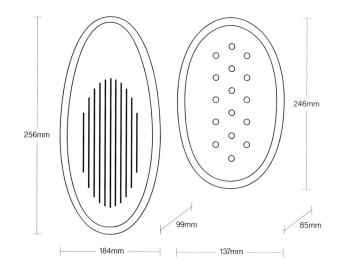

As if it were inflated, the diffuser gives to the touch. Easily removed, the negative track of the diffuser fits into the positive edge of the wall base.

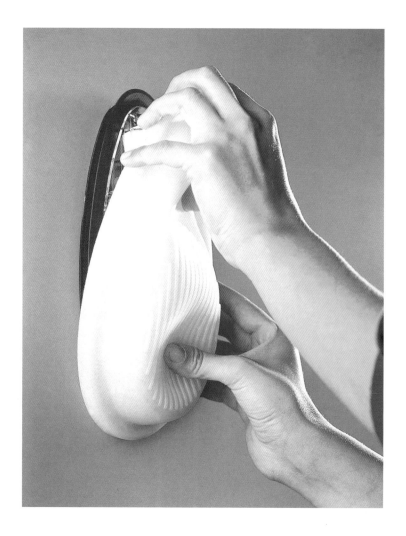

"Drop 1" and "Drop 2" sconces

The version with a
vertically ribbed
pattern is the "Drop 1."

The soft, malleable diffuser
is an injection-molded
silicon elastomer.

The wall-mounted base
is Lexan polycarbonate
(amber, blue, or green).

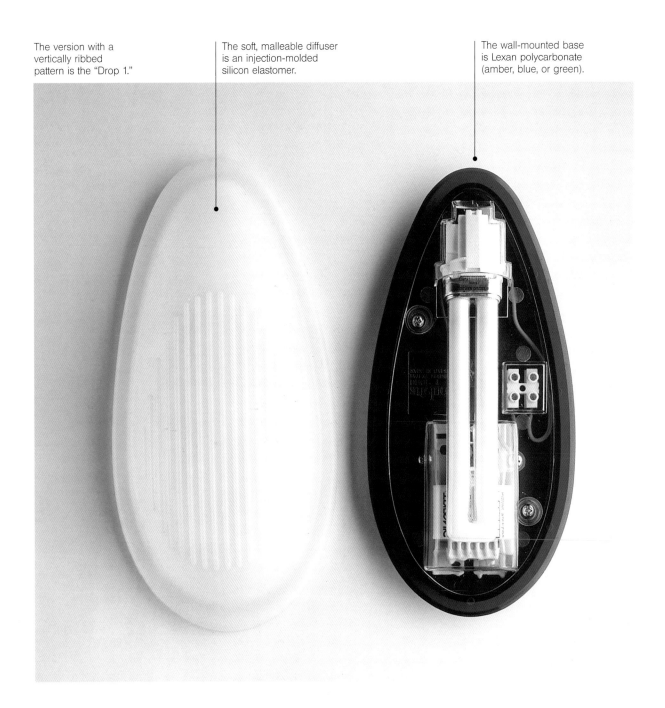

The version with a
pimple pattern is
the "Drop 2."

A soft light is projected through the diffuser and also,
due to the transparent nature of Lexan, through and
around the base onto the wall surface.

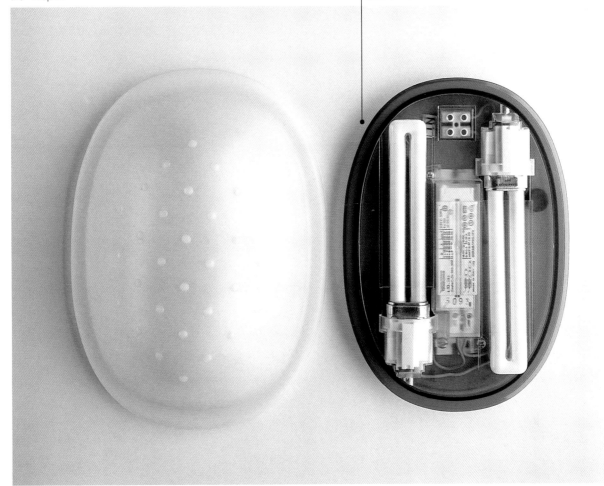

22

"Crinkle" table light

Designers: Lyn Godley (American, b. 1956)
and Lloyd Schwan (American, b. 1955)
Manufacturer: Godley-Schwan, Hamburg,
PA, U.S.A.
Date of design: 1996
Bulb: incandescent candelabra, 40w

This is a visually dynamic design for so simple
a solution. One square sheet of vividly colored
vinyl is heated and made into a somewhat
untidy shape, different for every example made.

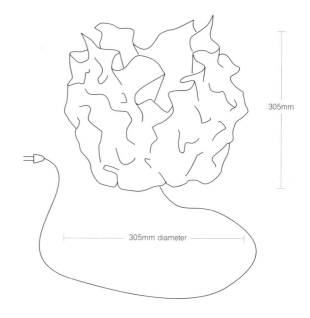

305mm

305mm diameter

A vinyl sheet (0.015mil) is heated and
hand-shaped into individually different
shapes. Available in white, yellow, pink
blue, green, red, and purple.

The diffuser is sand-
wiched between
heavy steel disks
(127mm diameter).

Candelabra bulb
(40w).

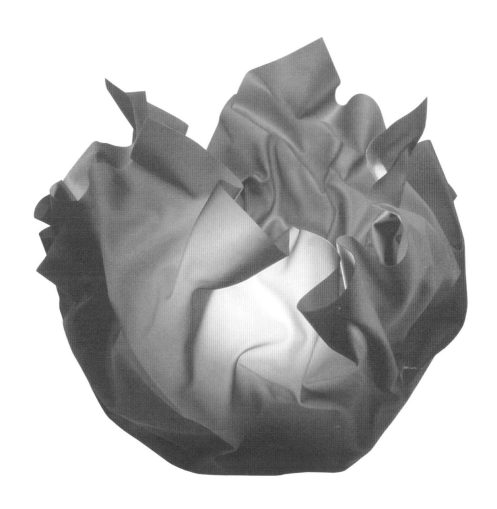

23

"Wall-A Wall-A" sconce

Designer: Philippe Starck (French, b. 1949)
Manufacturer: Flos S.p.A., Bovezzo (BR), Italy
Date of design: 1993
Bulb: compact fluorescent, 11w, 230v

This fixture reveals the sense of humor for which
this designer has become known and surreally
interprets a sconce; a traditional, if not corny,
lamp with a pleated fabric shade; and lighting
in general. The lamp incorporates the use of
technologically advanced materials.

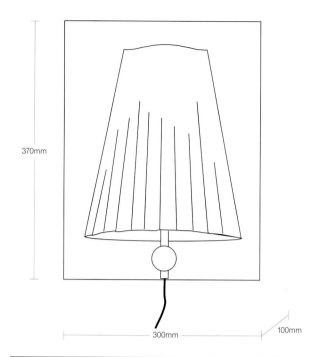

370mm

300mm

100mm

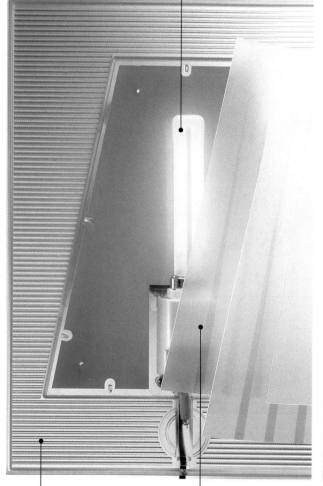

Compact halogen bulb
(11w, 220v).

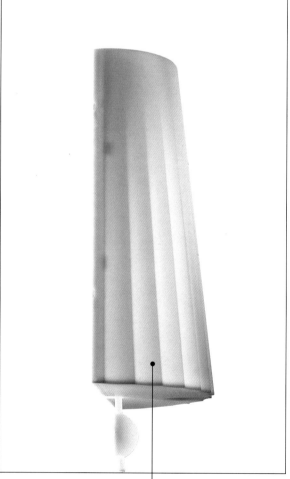

The background is a
striated thermoformed
technopolymeric sheet
(in transparent green,
black or terracotta).

Changeable filters
(in amber, azure, striped
red, striped green, or
transparent) provide
various lighting effects.

The diffuser, detachable
for maintenance and
filter changing, is
vacuum-formed
opaline polycarbonate.

24

"Soliel blanc" table light

Designer: Didier La Mache (French, b. 1945)
Manufacturer: the designer
Date of design: 1983
Bulb: Sylvania Circline O FC T9 CW, 222

Based on the designer's interest in the highly
esoteric aspects of geometry, this fixture,
which may be more sculpture than design, is
part of his ongoing involvement in symbolism
and archetypes which include the circle,
triangle, sphere, tetrahedron, pyramid, cube,
and convex surface.

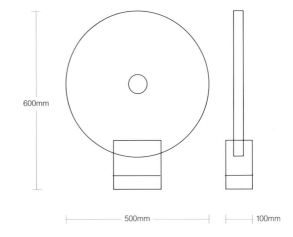

600mm

500mm   100mm

Three sets of bolts and nuts
and nylon washers support
the circular fluoresecent bulb
between the Plexiglas disks.

Circular fluorescent
lighting tube.

Two parallel disks in striped
metacrilate (Plexiglas).

Eslastomer disks act as
shocks to hold the large
diffuser disks in place.

Two rectangular glass
sections raise the
diffuser disks.

Two "U"-shaped bent steel
sheets (zinc plated) form
an open-ended box that
houses the transformer and
fluorescent-tube socket.

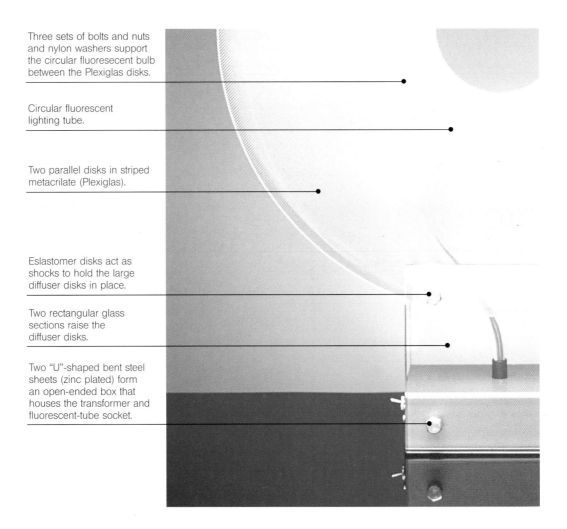

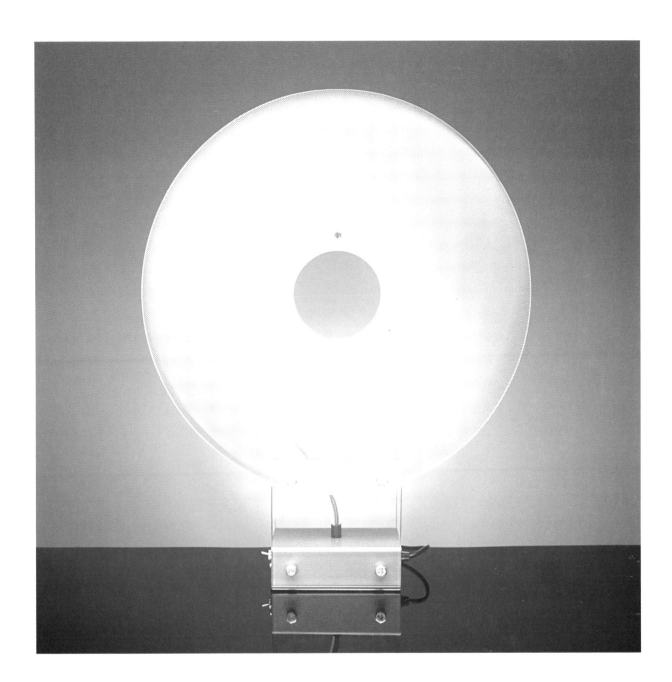

25

"Havana" hanging, wall, and floor light

Designer: Joseph Forakis (American, b. 1962)
Manufacturer: Foscarini Murano S.p.A., Murano (VE), Italy
Date of design: 1993
Bulb: E27 incandescent, 150w or energy saving 23w, 110/240v

This multipurpose lamp features a diffuser whose top segment is attached to the uppermost point of the central stem, leaving the other three segments to dangle. Of course, this feature is the most effective in the ceiling-hanging and wall models. The diffuser gives off a warm light from a cocoon-like container or as the title suggests, cigar-like. "Havana" makes reference to where some cigars are made. The segmented design permits easier shipment.

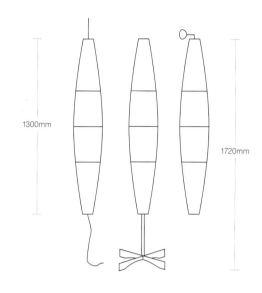

1300mm

1720mm

A metal armature (702mm high) (attached to the central post) holds the top diffuser segment aloft.

A second metal tubular armature houses the electrical cords.

Polyethylene diffuser (blue lines).

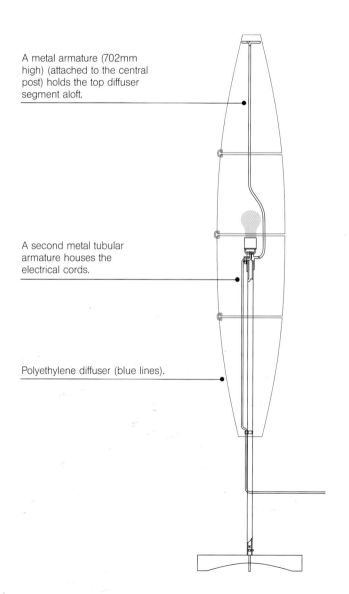

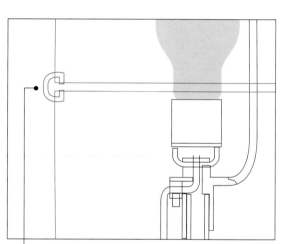

Clamps hold the four segments of the diffuser together, with some open spaces between the segments.

"Havana" hanging, wall, and floor lamp

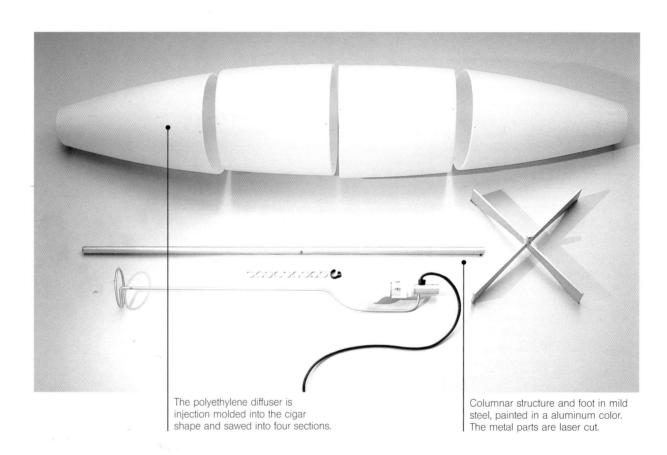

The polyethylene diffuser is injection molded into the cigar shape and sawed into four sections.

Columnar structure and foot in mild steel, painted in a aluminum color. The metal parts are laser cut.

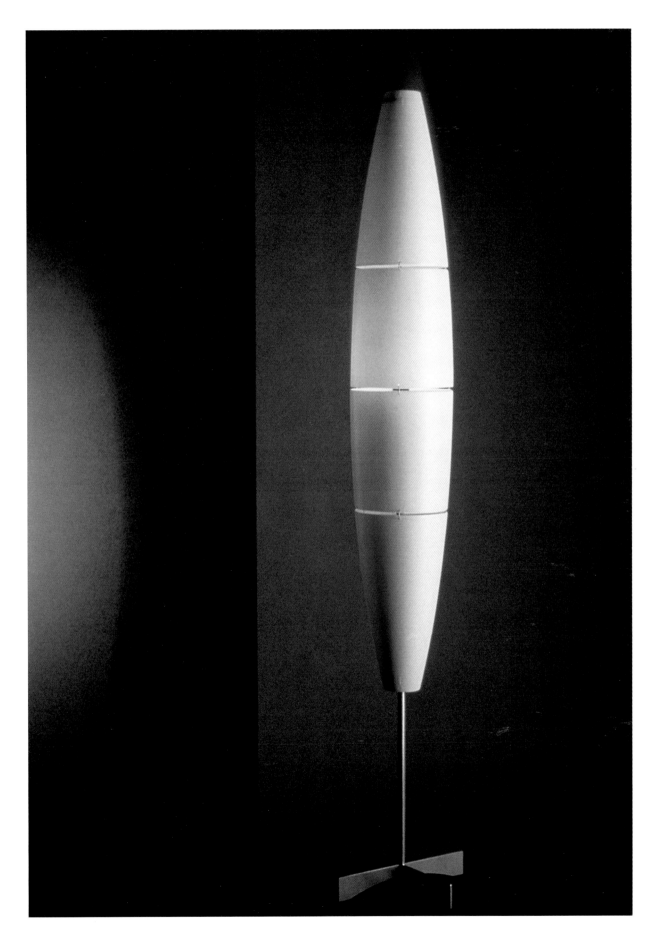

"Havana" hanging, wall, and floor lamp

Fibers and Composites

"Sirius Mushroom" hanging light

Designer: Russell D. Barker (British, b. 1972)
Manufacturer: Sirius Designs, High Wycombe, Buckinghamshire, Great Britain (distributed by SKK Lighting, London)
Date of design: 1994
Bulb: Spider fitting, E14 (Europe)/E12 (U.S.A./Japan), 60w, 110v, 230v, or 240v

Made by hand by the designer, the diffuser of this hanging lamp is a one-piece element. The decorative rubber balls may be removed and, according to the design, played with—an intentional design feature.

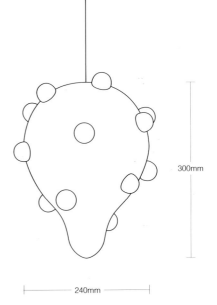

300mm

240mm

One of the two polyester resin molds used to form the diffuser.

A diffuser removed from the mold.

Fiberglass matting used for the reinforcement of the mold.

A finished and illuminated diffuser.

The colored rubber balls are inserted into holes made with a drill and may be removed at will.

The backside of the rubber balls can be seen inside the diffuser.

The ceramic socket is held in place via a wire armature.

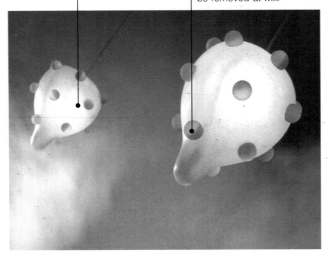

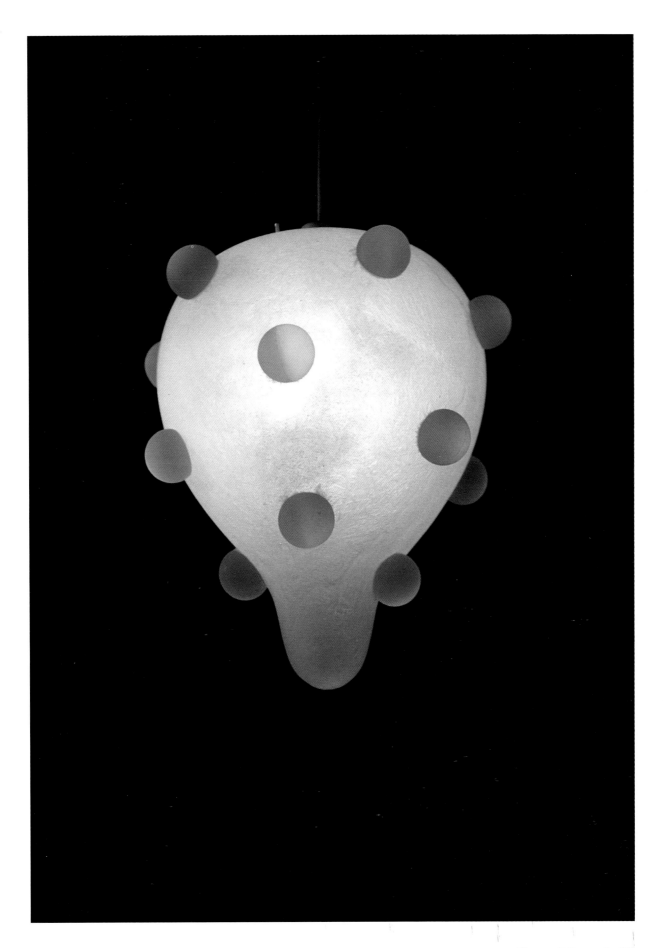

"E.T.A. Extraterrestrial Angel" floor light

Designer: Guglielmo Berchicci (Italian, b. 1957)
Manufacturer: Kundalini S.r.l., Milano, Italy
Date of design: 1997
Bulb: No. 1 Halotube, 150w; or No. 3 E14
incandescent, 40w; 11/220v

Through the use of various hand-driven production methods, this lamp is produced with a resin mold, injection molding, welding, laser cutting, and baking in a kiln. The result is an intriguing, very tall, slender fixture, in a range of bright colors, that features an interesting method for removing the central electrical column for easy maintenance.

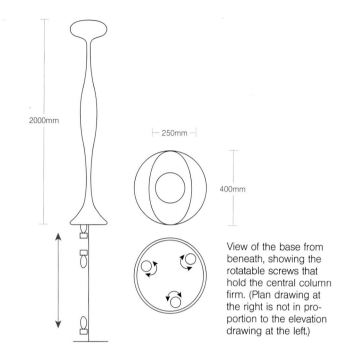

2000mm

250mm

400mm

View of the base from beneath, showing the rotatable screws that hold the central column firm. (Plan drawing at the right is not in proportion to the elevation drawing at the left.)

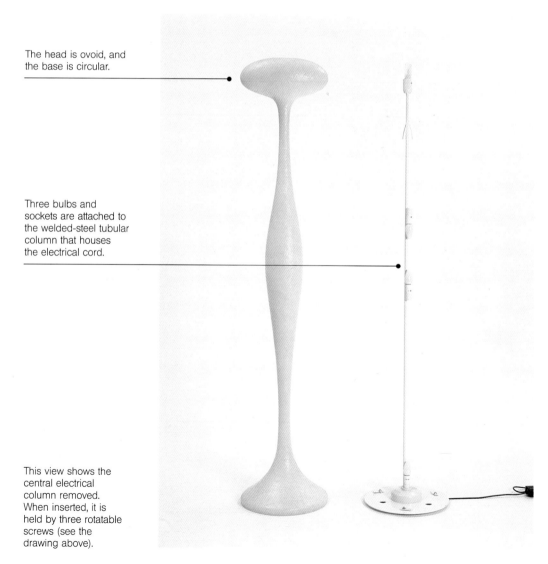

The head is ovoid, and the base is circular.

Three bulbs and sockets are attached to the welded-steel tubular column that houses the electrical cord.

This view shows the central electrical column removed. When inserted, it is held by three rotatable screws (see the drawing above).

"E.T.A. Extraterrestrial Angel"
floor light

A wooden model from which the mold is cast.

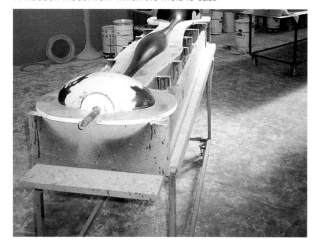

Sealed molds with the contents curing.

A craftsperson trims the polyamide body halves.

Fibreglass applied to both outside and inside the polyamide body.

The interior, after the fiberglass application, is being sealed.

On an assembled body, the base insert is applied.

Completed lamps are stored, and a craftsperson applies fiberglass.

The production process:
  The polyamide body is formed in two halves in a resin mold.
  The body is painted with a double protective kiln varnish.
  Special treatment makes the final resin non-toxic.
  The removeable base is attached to a welded steel column that supports the electrical cord and the three bulbs.

**"E.T.A. Extraterrestrial Angel"
floor light**

A disassembled fixture.

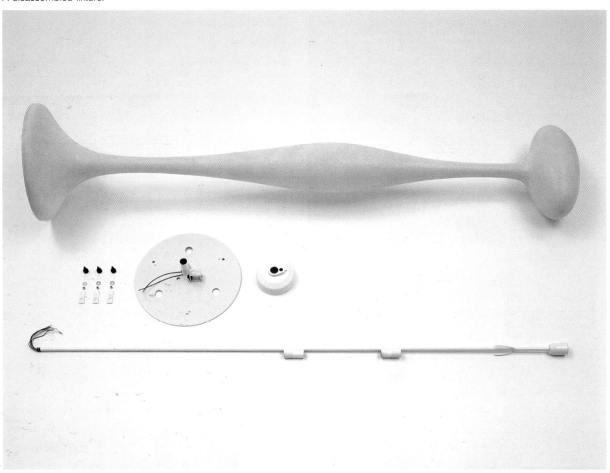

Glass

"Ondi di Luce"

Designers: Carlo Moretti (Italian, b. 1934)
with Marion Sterner (German, b. 1963) and
Wolfgang Sojer (German, b. 1962)
Manufacturer: Carlo Moretti S.r.l., Murano (VE), Italy
Date of design: 1993
Bulb: E14 incandescent, 60w, 220v

Created with materials produced by craftspeople in
the renowned glass-making area of Italy, this lamp
was configured in table, sconce, and ceiling versions.
The graceful use of glass tubes is reminiscent of
the best of European lighting of the 1920s and 1930s,
especially in France. The form of the lamp has been
compared by the designer to the distant rolling
undulation of the ocean at night.

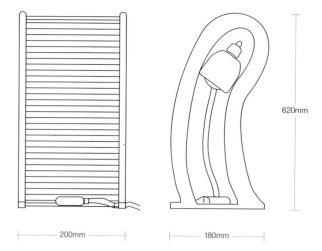

620mm

200mm   180mm

All versions of the frame,
into which the glass tubes
are fed, and the armature
are chromium-plated brass.

The large table lamp incorporates
80 internally etched glass tubes
(300mm long) and the small one
50 tubes (200mm long).

The glass tubes
are fed into the
brass frame.

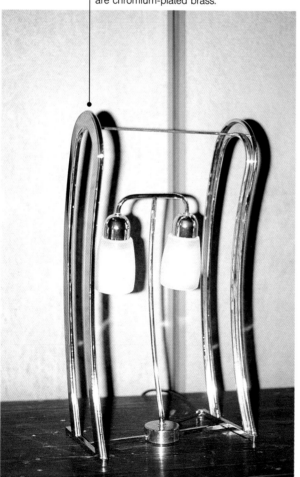

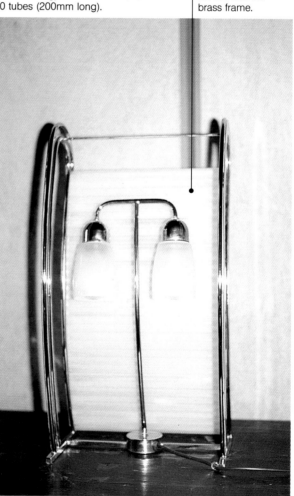

Glass/93

"Ondi di Luce"

The sconce includes 30 internally
etched glass tubes (200mm long).

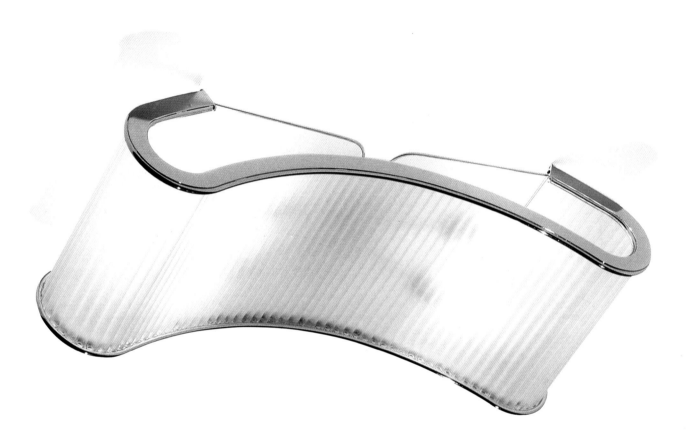

The ceiling-mounted model has 60 internally
etched Murano glass tubes (200mm long). In
none of the versions of the lamp is glue used
to hold the tubes which are fed into the inside
track of the frame.

29

"Velo" hanging and "Abavelo" table lights

Designer: Franco Raggi (Italian, b. 1945)
Manufacturer: Fontana Arte, Milano, Italy
Date of designs: "Velo" 1988, "Abavelo" 1990
Bulb: "Velo" R75 halogen, 150w, with regulation dimmer; "Abavelo" R7S halogen, 300w, class 1

These lamps exploit the flexible nature of glass, Resulting in fixtures with the appearance of being as light as air, but, in reality, quite heavy. In hanging, table-top, and wall versions, this light is an exercise in the manipulation possibilities of materials that, in this case, are traditional ones (glass and metal). The wall version is not shown.

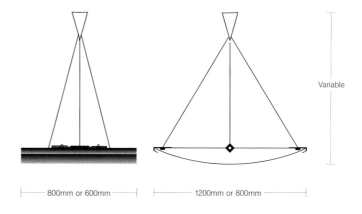

Variable

|← 800mm or 600mm →| |← 1200mm or 800mm →|

Elastic-like opaline glass is serigraphed in the central portion and bent like a bow. The outer edge is left clear. The table model features two parallel panes of glass.

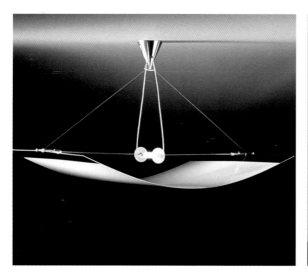

Cast aluminum base.

Electrical wires are fed through thin stainless-steel supports.

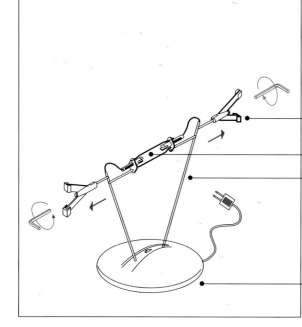

Pairs of metal fingers (two sets on the table model here and single ones on the hanging version above left) are attached with an Allen wrench and hold the glass-plate diffuser(s) in a bowed position.

Placement of the R7S halogen bulb.

Rod in chromium-plated brass or optical black.

The glass sheets (1.1mm thick) are chemically toughened and in the center sections serigraphed white. The table fixture dimensions are 500mm high, 500mm wide, and 200mm deep.

Base is polished die-cast aluminum.

30

"Milkbottle" hanging light

Designer: Tejo Remy (Dutch, b. 1960)
Manufacturer: DMD (Development Manufacturing
Distribution Rotterdam BV), Voorburg, The
Netherlands
Date of design: 1993
Bulb: E15, 15w, 220v

The distinction of this lighting fixture lies in its use
of a discarded everyday object and the unabashed
simplicity of its contrivance. The lamp was created
by one of the participants in the stable known as
Droog Design, the ad-hoc group which accents
a crafts approach to materials and the new
application of existing techniques. The carefully
preconsidered rigid parallel arrangement of the
wiring reveals a more purposeful ambience to
the fixture than it may have had otherwise. (See
another Droog design on pages 112–113.)

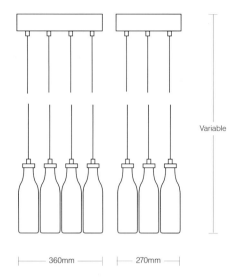

Variable

360mm   270mm

Standard round plastic-
covered elastic wiring.

Special stainless-steel caps
(not regular milk bottle ones)
hold the socket and bulb.

Twelve discarded milk
bottles, frosted on the
inside, offer ambient
lighting.

31

"Tesa" table light

Designer: Umberto Riva (Italian, b. 1928)
Manufacturer: Barovier & Toso Vetrerie Artistiche
Riunite S.r.l., Murano (VE), Italy
Date of design: 1985
Bulb: E27, 100w, 220v

This highly unusual lamp is obviously more
an artistic statement than a functional object,
although it does indeed provide light. Expensive,
precious, and carefully handmade, only a few
examples of this fixture were produced. All the
parts, pieces, and connectors are left exposed,
concealing no constructional secrets.

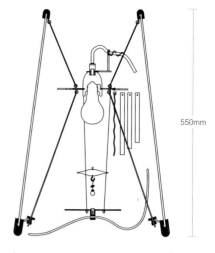

550mm

380mm diameter

The brass disk that holds the socket,
bulb, and glass pendants is suspended
in space within the cone by brass wires.

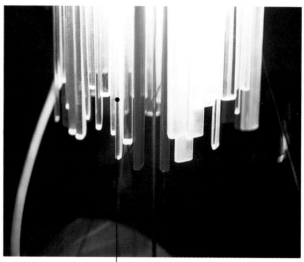

The dangling glass pendants (125mm,
140mm, and 155mm long) are wired
to the round socket disk through
holes in their tops.

Rubber shocks protect the top and bottom edges of
the glass cone onto which brass hooks and wires
hold the socket/bulb/pendant unit in suspension.

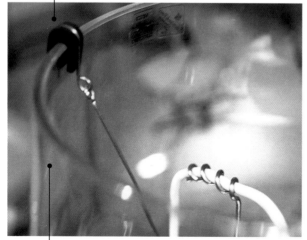

The conical outer
shell is transparent
mouth-blown glass,
cast in a die.

Metal parts
(brass) are
lathe cut.

Brass wire wrapped around the
white electrical cord firmly holds it
in certain bends, eliminating inter-
ference with the hanging pendants.

The triangular
base is brass.

32

"Ostrica in Orbita" hanging lights

Designer: Pepe Tanzi (Italian, b. 1945)
Manufacturer: Album S.r.l., Monza (MI), Italy
Date of design: 1996
Bulb: low-voltage halogen, 15w, 12v

This lamp takes advantage of a type of lighting design developed recently which features positive and negative electrical wires usually stretched across the length of the ceiling. By creating a frosted glass pill-shaped hollow diffuser with a narrow longitudinal mouth, the diffuser is held in space by the positive and negative wiring leads that are easily removed when slid to the center of the diffuser opening. (For a similar positive/negative wiring configuration, see pages 12–13.)

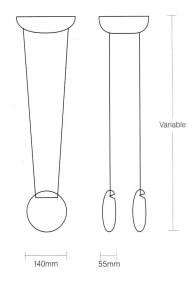

Variable

140mm   55mm

Bead stops—attached to the ends of the negative (on one side) and the positive (on the other side) electrical wires—hold the glass diffuser firmly.

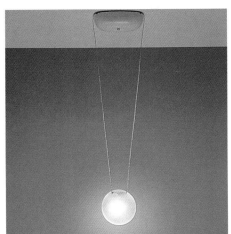

Bead stops slide to the sides of the diffuser slits and hold it securely aloft.

Low-voltage halogen bulb (15w, 12v) is suspended inside the glass diffuser.

Notice the parts of the mouth: wide for inserting the beads and the bulb and narrow for holding the beads.

The diffuser is mouth-blown, handmade, sand-etched borosilicate (high-heat-resistant) glass.

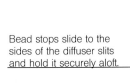

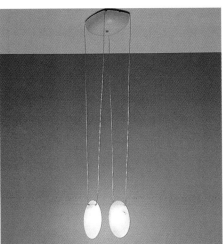

Single or double configurations are possible from a ceiling receptacle. Multiples can also be hung through the use of parallel ceiling wiring.

33

"Lamp with Switch"

Designer: Peter van der Jagt (Dutch, b. 1971)
Manufacturer: the designer
Date of design: 1996
Bulb: custom-blown glass, halogen, 15w, 220v

In a shape reminiscent of a 19th-century light bulb, this fixture may be far more important than its simple appearance belies. Revealing a lively imagination, the mechanics and engineering of this lamp are highly sophisticated. This fixture, more than a mere light bulb, is a commendable venture for a young designer. Except for the mouth-blown glass, all parts are standard elements purchased in a retail shop.

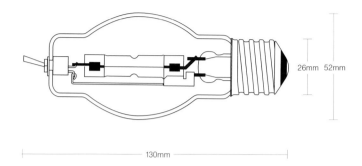

26mm 52mm

130mm

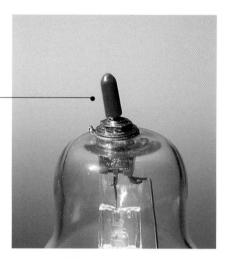

A sealed standard on/off switch (red vinyl over metal) protrudes through the glass.

Especially for this fixture, a mouth-blown glass bulb.

Halogen filament.

The bulb is sealed into the aluminum socket with a ceramic kit.

"Bolonia" table light

Designer: Josep Lluscá (Spanish, b. 1948)
Manufacturer: Metalarte S.A., Sant Joan Despi
(Barna), Spain
Date of design: 1987
Bulb: dichroic halogen, 20w, 12v

The form of this fixture, the designer suggests,
was inspired by old-fashioned bottles of water
capped with inverted drinking glasses that also
served as lids. The reflector, and thus the direction
of the light beam, swivels. Compare this example
with the metal-bodied lamp on pages 22–23.

400mm

140mm

The halogen bulb,
here pointing
downward, in the
holder which has
the appearance
of a bottle cap.

"Bolonia" table light

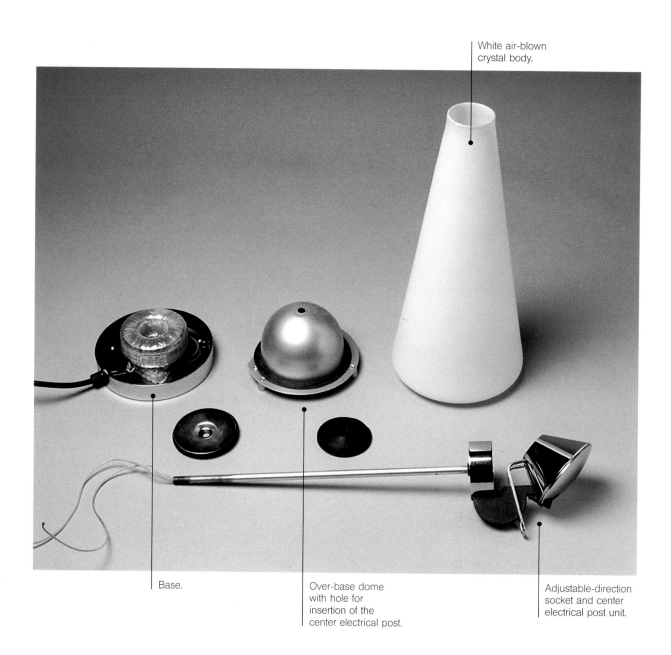

White air-blown crystal body.

Base.

Over-base dome with hole for insertion of the center electrical post.

Adjustable-direction socket and center electrical post unit.

Chrome ABS adjustable socket mounted to the central electrical-wiring post.

White air-blown crystal body.

Aluminum inner over-base element with hole for centerpost..

"Bolonia" table light

Lamps illustrate the full articulation
of the lighting projection.

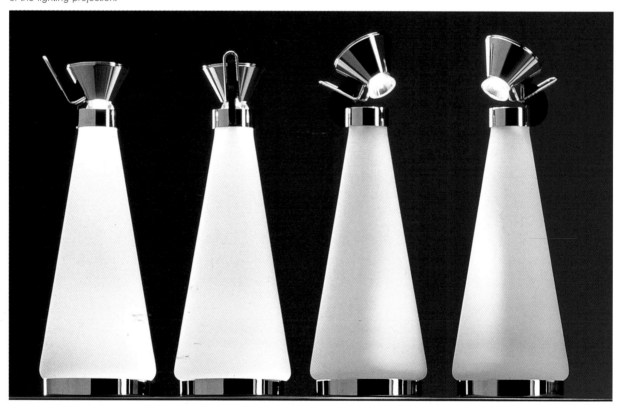

Paper

35

"Pop Up" light

Designer: Feddow Claassen (Dutch, b. 1970)
Manufacturer: DMD (Development Manufacturing Distribution Rotterdam BV), Voorburg, The Netherlands
Date of design: 1995
Bulb: E14 (Europe) or E12 (U.S.A., Japan)

Intentionally low-tech and inexpensive, this fixture features a brown corrugated-paper carton for its housing. When the carton is opened as one would ordinarily do by pulling on the lid and the flap, the bulb and socket elements are raised by hand. The bulb does not actually "pop up," and once raised cannot be inserted again. The designer is one of the members of the Droog Design group in Holland, who have become known for their witty, irreverent approach. (See another Droog fixture on pages 98–99.)

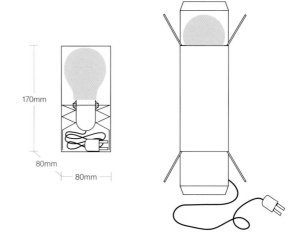

170mm

80mm

80mm

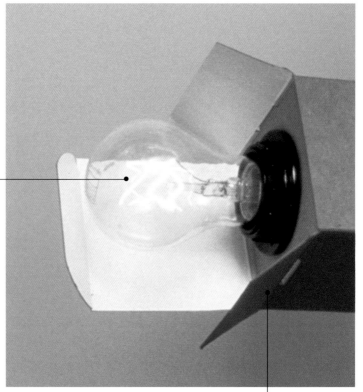

A clear light bulb, furnished with the carton, would possibly be more desirable frosted.

Employing standard electrical parts, black plastic gaskets (above and below the pop-up inside lid) hold the socket firmly.

An ordinary two-sided kraft-paper corrugated cardboard box houses the bulb and standard electrical parts.

36

"Light in the dark" sconce

Designer: Stevan Dohar (Hungarian, b. 1954)
Manufacturer: Adeline André Atelier, Paris, France
Date of design: 1995
Bulb: E14

The unusual appearance of the diffuser on this sconce is due to its being formed of a sheet of dried seaweed produced in Japan. The metal diffuser frame is held onto the metal wall frame with magnets, permitting easy detachment.

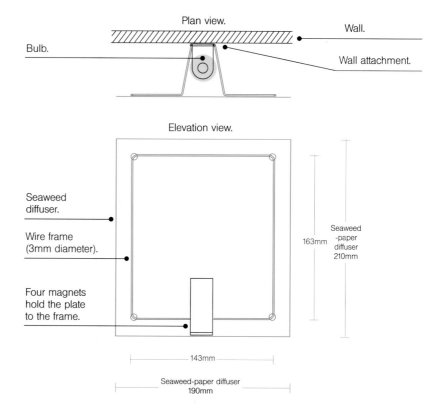

Plan view.

Bulb.

Wall.

Wall attachment.

Elevation view.

Seaweed diffuser.

Wire frame (3mm diameter).

Four magnets hold the plate to the frame.

163mm

Seaweed-paper diffuser 210mm

143mm

Seaweed-paper diffuser 190mm

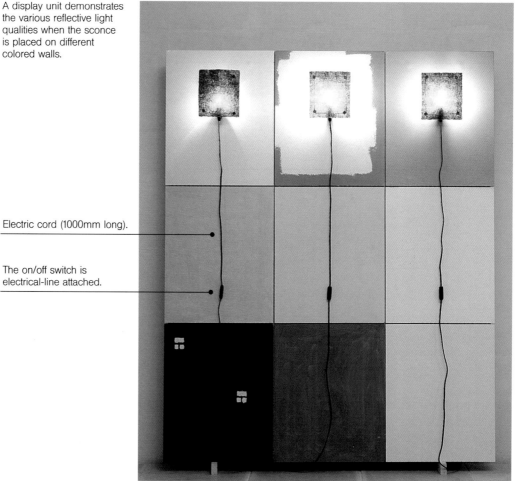

A display unit demonstrates the various reflective light qualities when the sconce is placed on different colored walls.

Electric cord (1000mm long).

The on/off switch is electrical-line attached.

37

"Image Light"

Designer: Simon Pont (British, b. 1950)
Manufacturer: Productivity, Exebridge,
Dulverton, Somerset, Great Britain
Date of design: 1995
Bulb: incandescent, 60w; or compact
fluorescent, 11w

This simple lighting fixture may concern the
intellectual messages printed on the bag than
the lamp itself. The intensity of the reflected
color emitted depends on the bag's color; for
example, orange is brighter than blue. This
inexpensive lamp, sold in a corrugated box, is
to be assembled by the end user following the
clear instructions printed on the box.

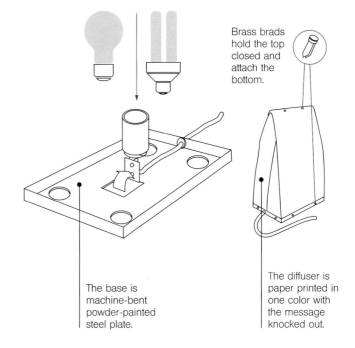

Brass brads
hold the top
closed and
attach the
bottom.

The base is
machine-bent
powder-painted
steel plate.

The diffuser is
paper printed in
one color with
the message
knocked out.

In a range of colors, the bag-diffusers
are printed with messages which
make references to various aspects of
light and range from glib words and
phrases, for example "Edison" and
"Aurora Borealis," to quotations, such
one by the 18th-century English poet,
William Blake, known to many English-
speaking people:
"Tiger, tiger burning bright
In the forest of the night,
What immortal hand or eye
Could frame thy fearful symmetry?"

38

"The Cheapest Light Possible" ceiling light

Designer: Constantin Boym (Russian, b. 1955)
Manufacturer: Boym Design Studio, New York, NY, U.S.A.
Date of design: 1985
Bulb: E14 (Europe), E12 (U.S.A., Japan)

This particular example of the lamp was made in 1997, though conceived almost a decade earlier. The designer's kitsch, throwaway sense of humor may be more expressive in this design than a concern for green issues. As its name reveals, the fixture is very inexpensive and may not offer as much aesthetic appeal as it does a realization of a fecund imagination.

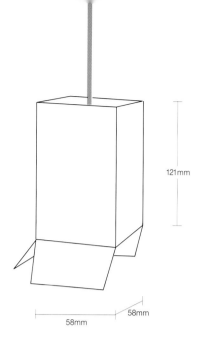

121mm

58mm

58mm

The diffuser is an original paper carton in which light bulbs are sold.

An aluminum foil lining protects the paper carton from the high heat of the bulb.

Electrical cord.

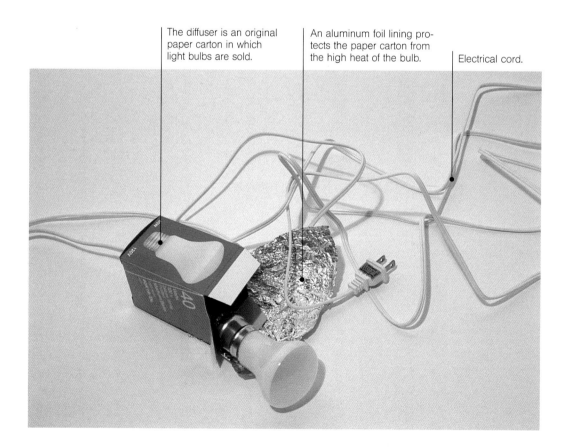

39

"Cálida" table and floor lights

Designer: Pete Sans (Spanish, b. 1947)
Manufacturer: Taller Uno DLC S.A., Camallera, Spain
Date of design: 1989
Bulb: P.L., 11w for the table version; incandescent, E27, 60w for the floor version; MEC 75 transformer

Due to the success of the floor version of this lamp, a table version was designed which employed the same materials and parts, except for the diffuser and base heights and the elimination of the bottom disk. A somewhat valuable material (brass or steel for the foot) has been combined with one of little worth (paper for the diffuser).

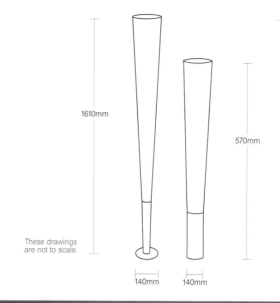

1610mm

570mm

These drawings are not to scale.

140mm   140mm

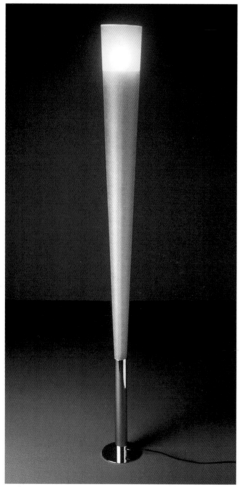

The floor version of "Cálida."

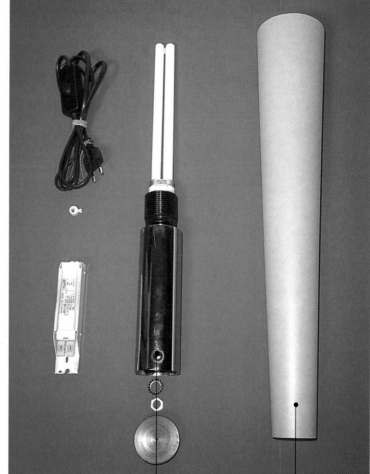

Foot is yellow brass (shown) or white chromium-plated steel.

The diffuser is plasticized paper.

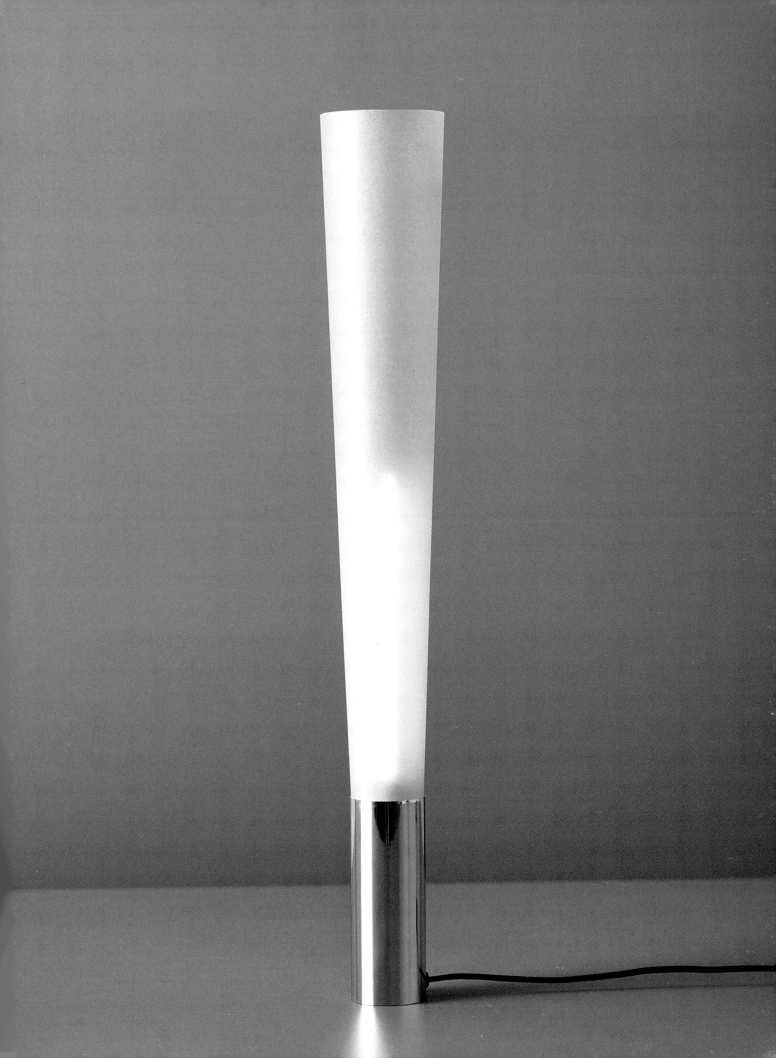

40

"Generation Two" lights

Designer: Roland Simmons (American, b. 1946)
Manufacturer: Interfold, Cowley, WY, U.S.A.
Date of design: 1995
Bulb: candelabra, 60w, 110/220v

These imposing fixtures, especially the tall models, are made of recycled corrugated paper. The end user assembles them, with a zipper, following the instructions provided with each lamp. They employ one to three bulbs depending on height.

After the end user attaches the center cord set to the base, the cocoon-like shell is closed by a zipper. (See bottom drawing.)

355mm x 1015mm   355mm x 1930mm   355mm x 2286mm

279mm x 915mm

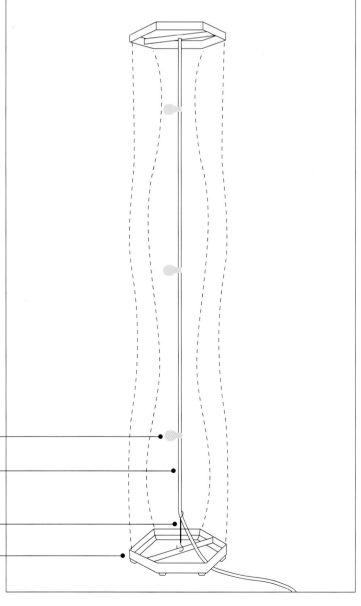

Tall model includes three bulbs.

Center cord set.

Elastic fastener holds the cord set taut.

White pinewood top and base.

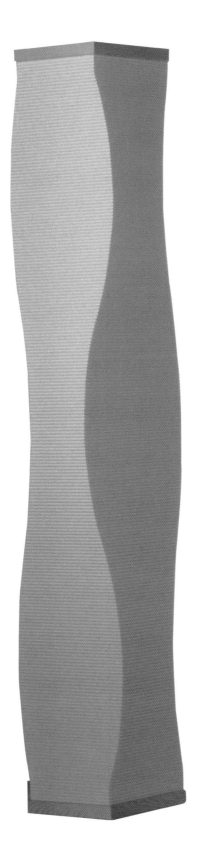

"Lamp Pack"

Designer: Tom Tilleul (French, b. 1967)
Manufacturer: Axis, Villejuif, France
Date of design: 1994
Bulb: E14 incandescent flame, 40w,
230/240v

The paper-bag-type body (or diffuser)
and the base stiffener of this lamp are
made of recycled paper products; even
the tie on the packaging is raffia. Created
by a member of a design cooperative,
this clever, witty, economical, and cheap-
to-ship fixture is easily assembled by
the end user.

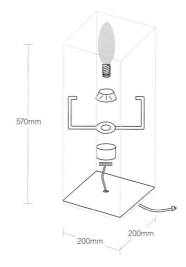

570mm

200mm

200mm

Square corrugated cardboard holds the already-
affixed socket and serves as a base stiffener.

Available in white (left) or
natural recycled paper.

The flat packaging is held together
with a raffia strand.

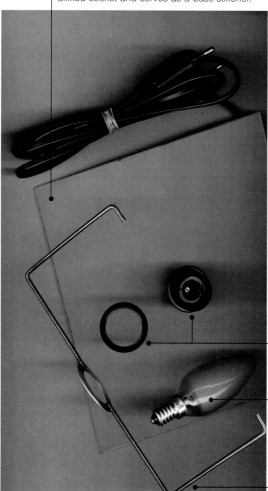

Socket and gasket.

E14 incandescent flame
bulb, 40w, 230–240v.

This welded brass device, held in
place by the socket and the screw-
on socket gasket, keeps the sides of
the bag-diffuser from touching the
bulb and thereby prevents burning.

42

"W&O" table light

Designer: Sasha Ketoff (Italian, b. 1949)
Manufacturer: Aluminor S.A., Contes, France
Date of design: 1984
Bulb: Halogen, 12v

The arm and diffuser of this lamp are rotatable
360°. For the square white reflector, the
designer used paper-coated foam core—
an inexpensive, non-durable, although easily
replaceable, material. The name "W&O" is
derived from "Wilbur & Orville," the Wright
brothers, suggesting that the thin support
structure of the fixture and its flat reflector
are structurally akin to the *Kitty Hawk* airplane.

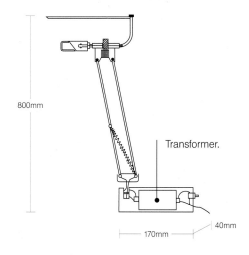

800mm

Transformer.

40mm

170mm

White paper-coated
foam core.

The artist's pencil sketch illustrates the
articulation of the arm and the reflector.

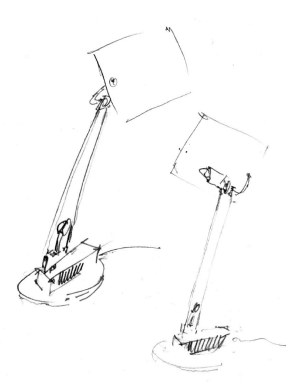

The arm and reflector holder are
tubular steel (8mm diameter).

The transformer is housed in the base
where the on/off switch is also located.

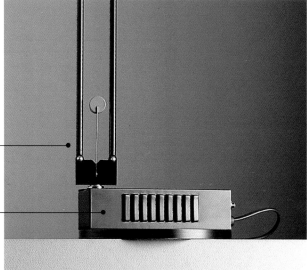

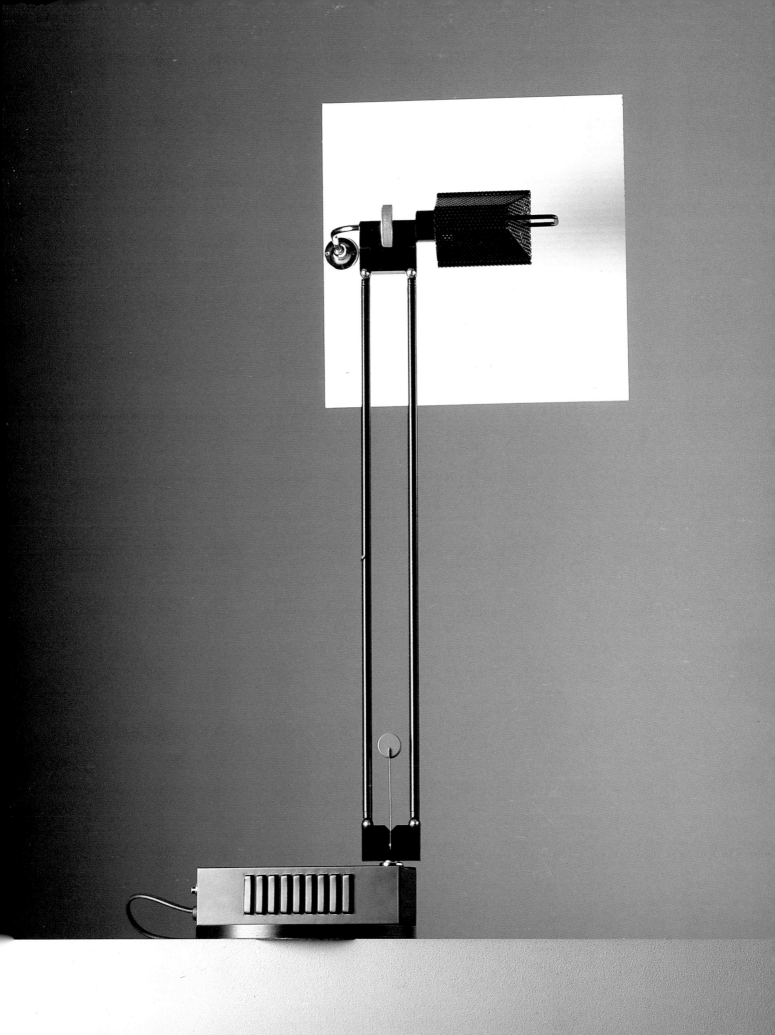

Textiles

43

"Lucilla" hanging and floor lights

Designer: Paolo Rizzatto (Italian, b. 1941)
Manufacturer: Luceplan S.p.A., Milano, Italy
Date of design: 1994
Bulb: A19 incandescent, 150w; compact fluorescent, 23w

A fixture inspired by traditional Asian lanterns, this lamp features high-tech fabric for the shade. Nomex is a flameproof fabric that can be brightly tinted; here it acts like a skirt hanging from a metal-rod frame. In order to create a stand for what is essentially a ceiling-hanging lamp, the designer conjured an insect-like frame.

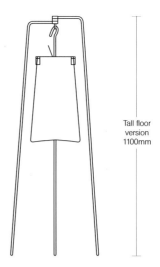

Tall floor
version
1100mm

Like a garment, the fire-proof Nomex fabric skirt (ecru, yellow, or red) is fitted onto the frame with the electrical cord inserted through a button-hole-like aperture.

On/off lever.

The wire frame/stand on both the ceiling and floor models is nickel-plated, bead-blasted steel rod (4mm).

"Lucilla" hanging and floor lights

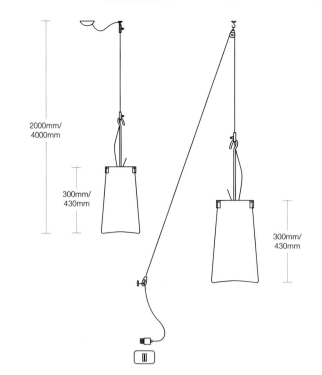

2000mm/
4000mm

300mm/
430mm

300mm/
430mm

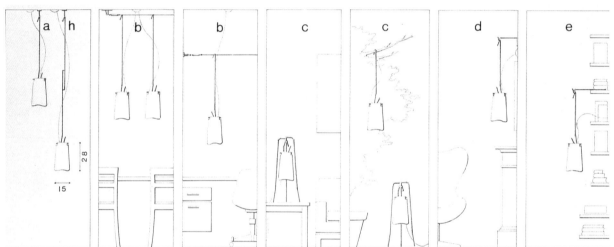

a h

28

15

b

b

c

c

d

e

One of the designer's drawings (above) reveals
his studies for various support solutions for wall
and ceiling mounting and surface placement.
(See the wall-mounted lamp on the facing page.)

In addition to the mounting hardware and
frames, this drawing shows the socket/bulb
cage. The top square rod surrounding the
bulb supports the Nomex shade and the
smaller square rod (below the bulb) holds
the fabric away from the bulb.

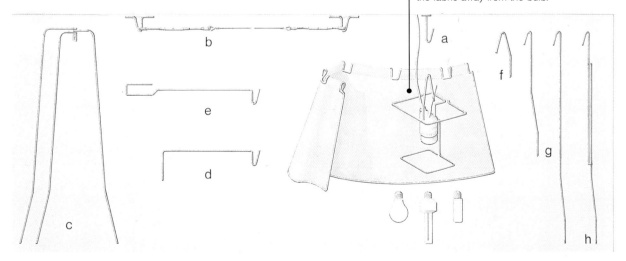

b

e

d

c

a

f

g

h

"Bombori" hanging light

Designer: Edward van Vliet (Dutch,
b. 1965)
Manufacturer: Equilibrium, Amsterdam,
The Netherlands
Date of design: 1996
Bulb: E14 incandescent, 75w, 220v

Ribbons and flaps control the light
emission on this highly unusual
textile lantern. Not only does light
project from the sides, it is also
cast through two colored or white
Plexiglas disks.

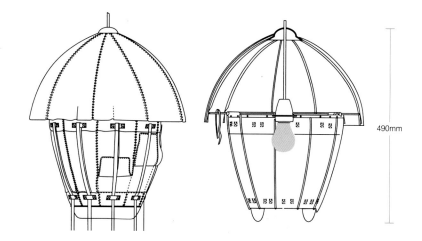

490mm

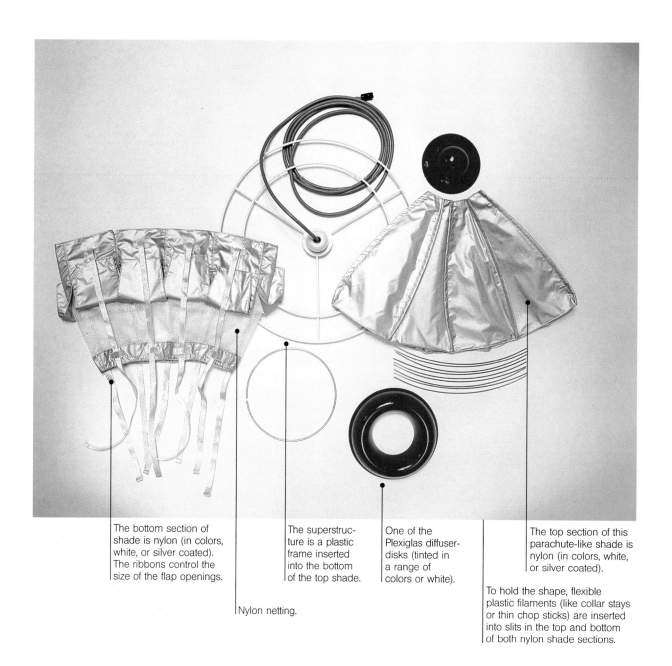

The bottom section of
shade is nylon (in colors,
white, or silver coated).
The ribbons control the
size of the flap openings.

The superstruc-
ture is a plastic
frame inserted
into the bottom
of the top shade.

One of the
Plexiglas diffuser-
disks (tinted in
a range of
colors or white).

The top section of this
parachute-like shade is
nylon (in colors, white,
or silver coated).

Nylon netting.

To hold the shape, flexible
plastic filaments (like collar stays
or thin chop sticks) are inserted
into slits in the top and bottom
of both nylon shade sections.

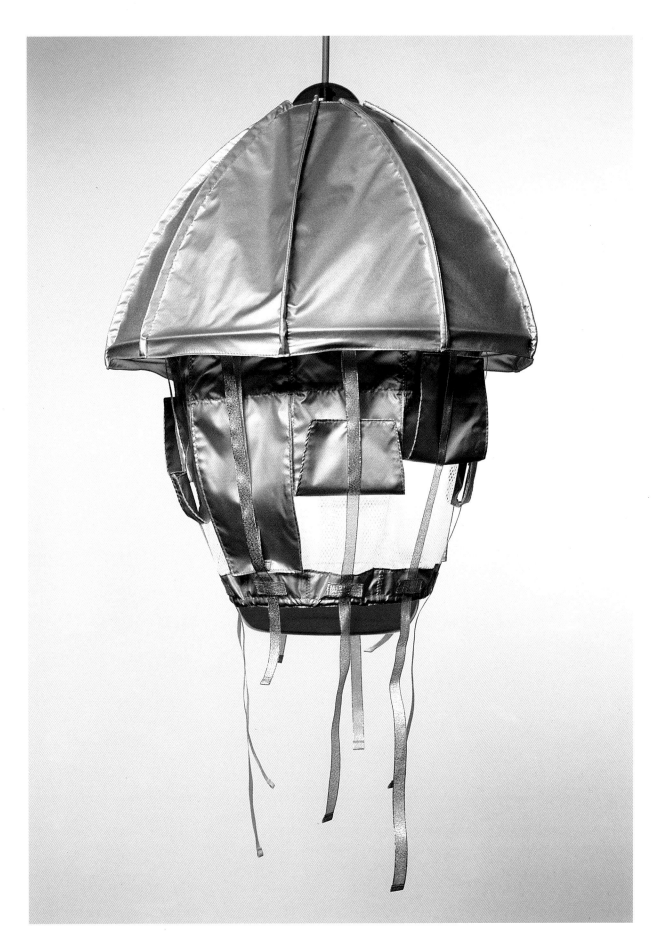

"Filumena" hanging light

Designer: Mark R. Anderson (American, b. 1964)
Manufacturer: prototype by Pasquale e Salvatore De Maio S.n.c., Caserta (NA), Italy
Date of design: 1996
Bulb: 100–150w Halogen frosted E27 socket type, 110 or 220v

Designed to be reminiscent of the laundry hanging over passage ways in small Southern Italian towns, the linen panels on this fixture are furnished with an accessory hook attached to a thin plastic coated steel line which can pull the drapery aside. This prototype was produced for the occasion of the exhibition "Progetti e Territori '96" held at the Abitare Il Tempo furniture fair in Verona, Italy, where the lamp was handwrought by artisans in the area.

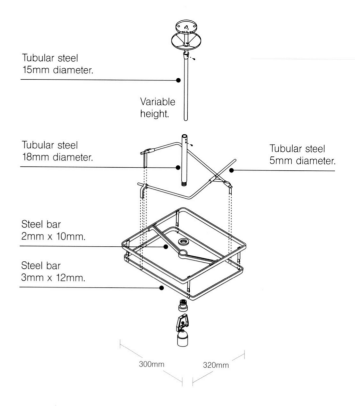

Tubular steel 15mm diameter.

Variable height.

Tubular steel 18mm diameter.

Tubular steel 5mm diameter.

Steel bar 2mm x 10mm.

Steel bar 3mm x 12mm.

300mm   320mm

Linen panels, like clothes drying on a line, are fed onto bent steel bars.

The bare wrought-iron frame, absent of the linen hangings.

45

"Filumena" hanging light

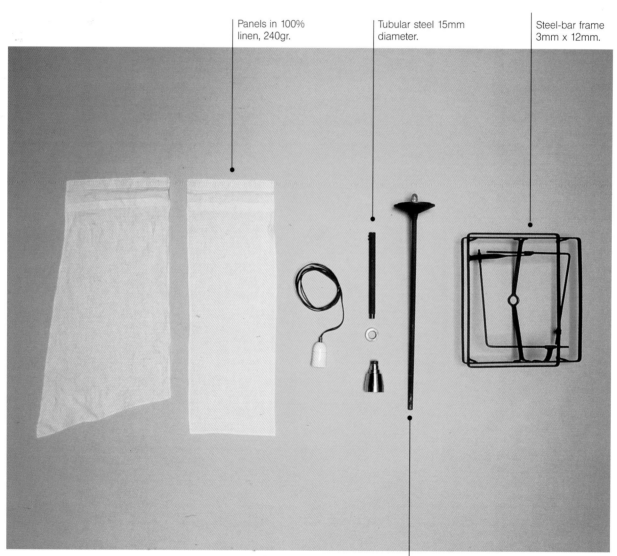

Panels in 100% linen, 240gr.

Tubular steel 15mm diameter.

Steel-bar frame 3mm x 12mm.

The center coupling and the bulb holder are nickel plated with a satin finish.

Center support: steel tube.

Metal parts are polyurethane single-coat painted over a tinted primer.

Wood, Ceramics, and Other Materials

46

Table light

Designer: Theodore S. Abramczyk
(American, b. 1959)
Manufacturer: the designer
Date of design: 1996
Bulb: Satco tubular 40w, 120v

Traditional in concept, the departure here
is the deftly manipulated thin-wood veneer
which gives off a warm light, either in its
natural light color or tinted orange. The
lamp, which floats above the metal plate,
is available in two colors.

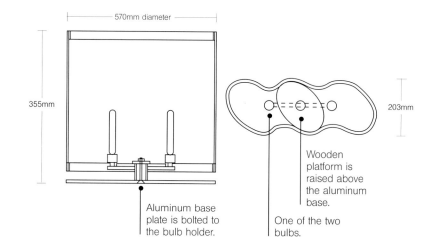

570mm diameter

355mm

203mm

Aluminum base
plate is bolted to
the bulb holder.

Wooden
platform is
raised above
the aluminum
base.

One of the two
bulbs.

The orange color version;
the natural color is shown
on the facing page.

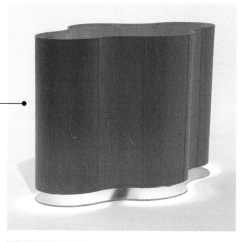

Top and bottom of the
veneer diffuser are glued to
a wooden support ring.

One thickness of wood
veneer (sanded, spray-
painted with varnish, and
polished) forms the diffuser.

Sheet aluminum base
plate conforms to the
silhouette of the diffuser.

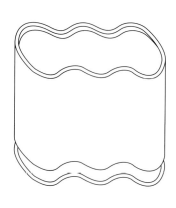

47

"George" floor light

Designers: reflector unit, Tobias Grau (German, b. 1957); tripod, Florian Borkenhagen (German)
Manufacturer: Tobias Grau GmbH + Co.
Hamburg, Germany
Date of design: 1996
Bulb: B15d, 100w; without transformer, high-voltage

The tiltable spotlight on this fixture can also be rotated, and the light beam can be dimmed and adjusted from a reflector beam to a narrow spot. The light is projected directly or, with the stretched-cloth screen, indirectly.

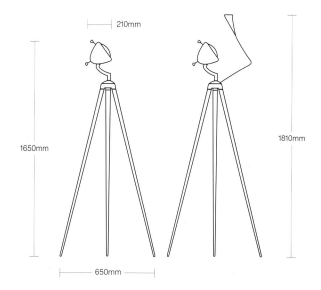

Reflective fabric, to create indirect lighting, is mounted onto a metal-rod frame.

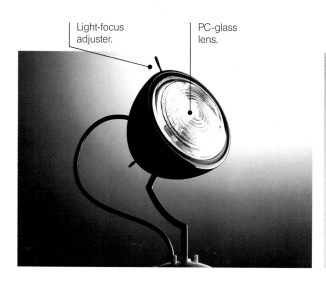

Light-focus adjuster.

PC-glass lens.

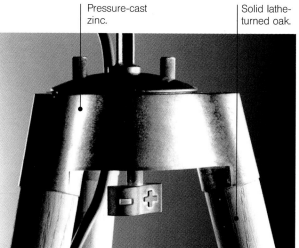

Pressure-cast zinc.

Solid lathe-turned oak.

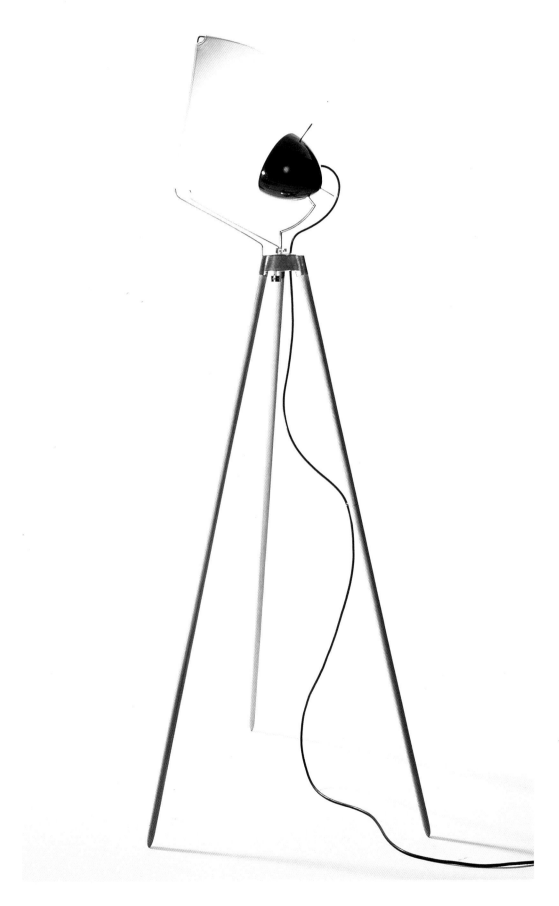

"Living Lighting"

Designer: Harry Allen (American, b. 1964)
Manufacturer: Selee Corporation, Hendersonville, NC, U.S.A.
Date of design: 1994
Bulb: tubular incandescent, 25–75w, 120v

While working on a lamp project, the designer discovered that ceramic foam, when held up to the light, was translucent. Through the patient cooperation of an empathetic manufacturer, he was able, in his own words, "to make such a crazy idea work."

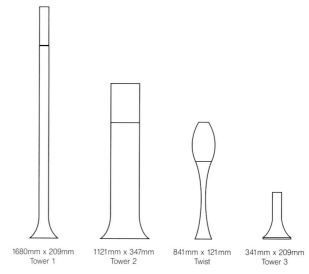

1680mm x 209mm
Tower 1

1121mm x 347mm
Tower 2

841mm x 121mm
Twist

341mm x 209mm
Tower 3

Ceramic foam is fired in a kiln, drilled or sawed (like marble) into various shapes at the industrial ceramics plant, and then shipped to the designer who attaches the porous ceramic diffuser to the base.

The base is welded sheet metal, later painted.

The electrical parts are screwed into the base.

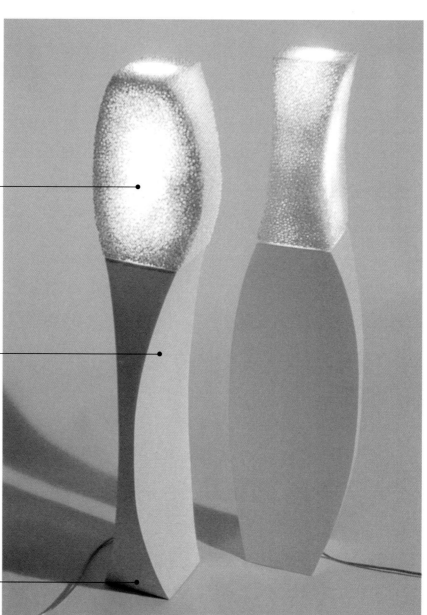

"Living Lighting"

The array of heights and shapes made possible by the manipulation of ceramic foam (for the diffusers) and welded sheet metal (for the bases).

The Selee ceramic material is formed when open-cell polyurethane foam is infused with various oxides, ranging from compounds of yttrium, zirconium, and other materials to alumina. This particular fixture employed Selee A which contains only aluminum oxide. Baked in a high-temperature kiln, the process eliminates the polyurethane and produces a substance with the appearance of sea coral.

The production process below at the Selee Corporation plant in Hendersonville, NC, does not specifically illustrate the foam forms used in Harry Allen's fixtures but the procedure is the same.

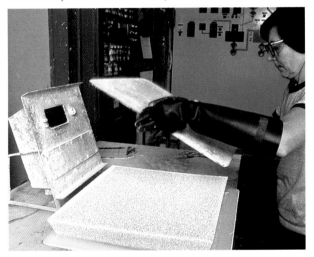

A gloved worker inspects "green" (prior to firing) ceramic foam.

A ceramic foam slab is being trimmed.

Sheets of ceramic foam enter the kiln.

Conveyor belt operation of ceramic foam exiting the kiln.

"T41" sconce and "T43" hanging light

Designer: Luke Gurney (British, b. 1964)
Manufacturer: the designer
Date of design: 1989
Bulbs: E14 incandescent, 240v, round or flame shaped

Here are two lamps that, by utilizing everyday objects recognizable by everyone, serve both utility and whimsey. Real undecorated cups, saucers, and a teapot were drilled through, and brass tubing was bent into the kind of flowing forms, including the hanging chain and ceiling fitting, found in English and Flemish 17th- and 18th-century candle-fitted lighting fixtures.

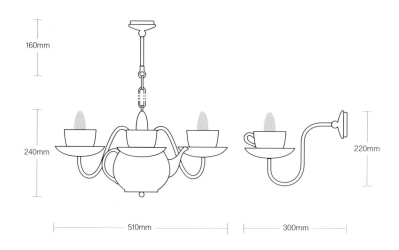

Nickle-plated brass tubing.

Ceramic cups, saucers, and teapots were drilled through to accommodate the fittings. The ceiling finial is the teapot cover.

"The Lamp"

Designer: Alexander Gelman (Russian, b. 1967)
Manufacturer: 555 Gallery, Jersey City, NJ, U.S.A.
Date of design: 1996
Bulb: quartz, 250w

Not a lamp at all but rather a metaphor, this image has been created by projecting light over a painted image on a wall. The design was originally drawn by the artist for a poster advertising a poetry reading.

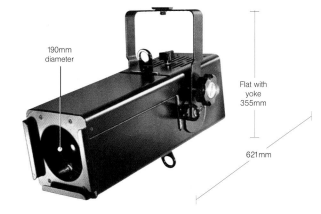

190mm diameter

Flat with yoke 355mm

621mm

Mounted on the ceiling, a 152mm zoom elliptical pattern two framing projector (250w) casts the white shade shape onto the wall. The image is precisely placed to match up with the black "base."

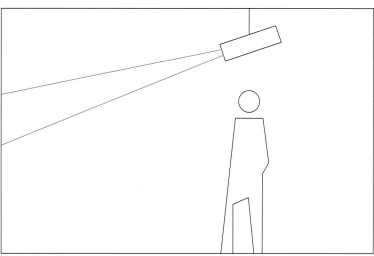

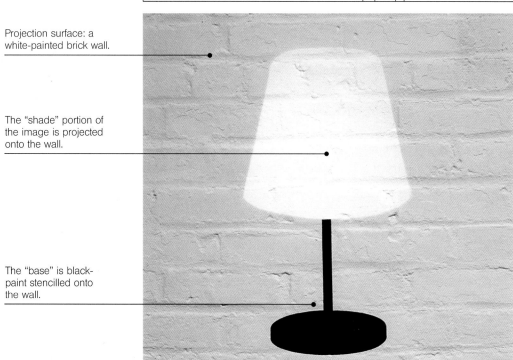

Projection surface: a white-painted brick wall.

The "shade" portion of the image is projected onto the wall.

The "base" is black-paint stencilled onto the wall.

Indices

Designers

Manufacturers

General Index

Acknowledgments

The Pro–Design series was developed from an original idea by Jean Koefoed.

The following people were very helpful in the preparation of this book. Its value, if any, is due to their generous assistance and also that of the manufacturers' representatives and designers whose works are discussed here.

Paola Antonelli, The Museum of Modern Art
Arlette Barré-Despond
Harriet Bee, The Museum of Modern Art
George M. Beylerian, Material Connexion
Dr. Claire Bonney
Isabelle Denamur
Olivier Gagnère
Arlene Hirst, *Metropolitan Home*
Ivan Luini, Luceplan USA Inc.
Murray Moss, Moss
Dianne H. Pilgrim, Cooper-Hewitt National Design Museum
Christa Schumann, Aero
Stephen Van Dyk, Cooper-Hewitt National Design Museum Library

Permissions

Photography and artwork was generously provided by the following contributors, preceded by page numbers:

12–13 Jorge Pensi/B.Lux
14–15 Garcia Garay
16–19 Donald Stählin
20–21 Lucitalia S.p.A./Studio Azzurro (photog.)
22–23 Gaspar Glusberg
24, 26–29 Luxo Italiana S.p.A./ Isao Hosoe
25 Zagnac (photog.)
30–32 Metalarte S.A./Sergi and Oscar Devesa i Bajet
34–37 Kundalini S.r.l.
38–41, 43 Louis Poulsen & Co. A/S
42 Louis Poulsen & Co. A/S; Planet/Bent Ryberg (photog.)
44–45 Marc Harrison
46–47 ISM Objects
48 Inflate
49 Inflate/Jason Tozer (photog.)
50–51 Goldman Arts, Inc.
52–53 Martins and de Oliveira
54 (bottom) Jean-Marie Massaud (illus.)
55 Jean-Marie Massaud/V.I.A.
56–59 Luceplan/Alberto Meda
60–61 Ross Tuthill Menuez
62–63 Christophe Pillet
64 Sculpture-Jeux S.A./ Christian Horrenberger (photog.)
65 Sculpture-Jeux S.A.
66–67 Samuel Parker S.r.l./Michele Salmi, Mario Tagliabue (photogs.)
68–71 Flos S.p.A.
72–73 Godley-Schwan
74–75 Flos S.p.A.
76–77 Didier La Mache
79, 81, 82 Foscarini Murano S.p.A./ Emilio Tremocada (photog.)
80–82 Foscarini Murano S.p.A./ Roberto Baldassarri (photog.)
84–85 Russell D. Baker
86–87, 90 Kundalini S.r.l./ Carlo Lavatori (photog.)
88–89 Kundalini S.r.l.
92–95 Carlo Moretti S.r.l.
96–97 Fontana Arte/Franco Raggi
98–99 DMD (Development Manufacturing Distribution Rotterdam BV)/Hans van der Mars (photog.)
100 Cinzia Anguissola d'Altoé
101 Barovier & Roso Vetrerie Artistiche Riunite S.r.l.
102–103 Album S.r.l.
104–105 Peter van der Jagt
106–110 Metalarte S.A./Josep Lluscá
112–113 DMD (Development Manufacturing Distribution Rotterdam BV)/ Hans van der Mars (photog.)
114 Adeline André Atelier
115 Toshi Fugii (photog.)
116–117 Productivity/Simon Pont
118–119 Boym Design Studio
120–121 Taller Uno DLC S.A./Pete Sans
122–123 Interfold/Roland Simmons
124 (bottom right)–125 Axis
126–127 Sacha Ketoff
130–133 Luceplan S.p.A.
134–135 Equilibrium/Edward van Vliet
136–138 Daniele Piccin (photog.)
140–141 Theodore S. Abramcyk
142–143 Tobias Grau
144–146 Harry Allen
147 Selee Corporation
148–149 Luke Gurney
150–151 Alexander Gelman (photog.)